CARV

George Mackay Brown (1921–96) was one of the twentieth century's most distinguished and original writers. His lifelong inspiration and birthplace, Stromness in Orkney, moulded his view of the world, though he studied in Edinburgh at Newbattle Abbey College, where he met Edwin Muir, and later at Moray House College of Education. In 1941 he was diagnosed with pulmonary tuberculosis and lived an increasingly reclusive life in Stromness, but he produced, in spite of his poor health, a regular stream of publications from 1954 onwards. These included *The Storm* (1954), *Loaves and Fishes* (1959), *A Calendar of Love* (1967), *A Time to Keep* (1969), *Greenvoe* (1972), *Hawkfall* (1974), *Time in a Red Coat* (1984) and, notably, the novel *Beside the Ocean of Time* (1994), which was shortlisted for the Booker Prize and won the Saltire Book of the Year.

His work is permeated by the layers of history in Scotland's past, by quirks of human nature and religious belief, and by a fascination with the world beyond the horizons of the known.

He was honoured by the Open University and by the Universities of Dundee and Glasgow. The enduringly successful St Magnus Festival of poetry, prose, music and drama, held annually in Orkney, is his lasting memorial.

GEORGE MACKAY BROWN

Carve the Runes:
Selected Poems

Edited by

Kathleen Jamie

This selection published in Great Britain in 2021 by
Polygon, an imprint of Birlinn Ltd

Birlinn Limited
West Newington House
10 Newington Road
Edinburgh EH9 1QS

9 8 7 6 5 4 3 2 1

www.polygonbooks.co.uk

ISBN 978 1 84697 516 5
eBook ISBN 978 1 78885 467 2

British Library Cataloguing-in-Publication Data
A catalogue record for this book is available from the British Library.

Typeset by Hewer Text UK Ltd, Edinburgh
Printed and bound in Great Britain by Clays Ltd, Elcograf S.p.A.

Contents

from *The Year of the Whale* (1965)

from *Fishermen with Ploughs* (1971)

Introduction

In his scant, posthumous autobiography George Mackay Brown tells us how, as a young man and a committed drinker, he frequented pubs, listened to yarns and discovered that 'under the drab surface complexities, there exists a ritualistically simple world of joy and anger'. He quit drinking, but took this revelation forward into his creative life: it was an idea he cleaved to and developed. What Brown sought in his poetry and stories' work was ritual, enduring and returning powers. It was an unfashionable stance in the mid twentieth century, but for Brown it was an empowering one.

The 'drab surface complexities' he had least interest in were his own; he was in no way concerned with self-revelation, or self-exploration. In fact, the first-person singular is almost entirely absent in his work, unless used by a persona. A rare exception is his elegy for his father, and his father's lifeway, 'Hamnavoe'. (Hamnavoe was the Viking name for the harbour town now called Stromness, Brown's native place.) This erasure of the self functioned as a stepping-back in order to see better into the lives and rituals of others. It allowed him to become a craftsman.

From the outset, even as a young man, his poetry concerned itself with his island home. Indeed, almost the first line Brown ever published was 'For the islands I sing'. Rather than confessions, he wrote what Douglas Dunn called 'documentary lyrics'. His concerns were the ancestral world, the communalities of work, the fables and religious stories which he saw as underpinning mortal lives. Even in his first collection, *The Storm*, published in 1954 when he was thirty-three, these poetic concerns were already laid out: his *dramatis personae* already in place, fishermen and farmwives. There already is the crofting year, the voyaging, the figures from the near-mythic past. Brown believed from the outset that poets had a social role and his true task was to fulfil that role. This is not the attitude of a shrinking violet, tentatively exploring his 'voice'. Art was sprung from the community, and his role as poet was to know that community, to sing its stories. But there was also room for introspection; the poet's task was simultaneously to 'interrogate silence'.

The islands, for which he sang, were of course, those of the Orkney archipelago. It's well known that Brown spent almost all of his life in the harbour town of Stromness, finding there more than enough of symbols and stories, images, characters and history to sustain a long creative career. Following his mother's death, he lived alone. He never married, but he enjoyed the muse-company of spirited young women such as Stella Cartwright of Edinburgh, to whom he was briefly engaged; in later life he may have had an affair or two. There were no children. He had plenty of friends and correspondents. He may or may not have been shy in his private life. (Shy, or irritated by interruptions in his true task? Solitary, or adept at finding ways not to be distracted?) In later years he occupied a small ex-council flat, which served as a harbour from where his imagination ranged in time and space. A storyteller, novelist and dramatist as well as a poet, in one sense he was very much of the twentieth century, in that he was born after the First World War, in 1921, and died just as the century was closing in 1996. Ill health was his life's companion; he had tuberculosis, but it spared him from being conscripted in the Second World War, and helped save him from tiresome travels or day-jobs. In one sense he went nowhere, in another, he knew exactly where he was going. Writing was his self-rescue from a life of pained listlessness. A disciplinarian, he wrote every day at his small table, in pen and ink. But his imagination wasn't an easy escape: it brought its own travails. He was subject to depression and fatigue.

Brown's champions and critics alike all feel obliged to address his island-dwelling. Some critics did sniff at what they misheard as wistfulness or feyness, and regarded his Orkney-universe as limiting. But for Brown, Orkney was enabling. For him, cyclical, liturgical or agricultural stability was enabling. (It is this stability of place and attitude which is both beguiling and frustrating to some modern readers, who may misread in it a political conservatism.) At a time when many in Scotland had left the land and their native parishes, for good reason or ill, and had become a proletariat, Brown was blessed in having a place of his own, and finding that place a boundless resource. He neither escaped from Orkney nor escaped to it. As he put it himself, in 'Fisherman and Boy':

> you will learn more in Orkney
> than Mansie did
> who made seven salt circles of the globe

(Note that kenning, the 'salt circles', and the number seven – ever the magic, resonant number.) Or, as his admirer Seamus Heaney put it: 'He transforms everything by passing it through the eye of the needle of Orkney.' And of course, Brown wrote in English, a global language. Accented English, island English maybe, but he did not write in Scots or

Orcadian dialect. With English as his chosen medium, he could reside in Stromness and speak to the world. As master of such a language, he was not so isolated or remote as some like to believe.

Furthermore, even if Brown's world was limited geographically (an accusation hard to sustain under the vast skies and ocean horizons of his archipelago), it was not limited in time. Like his novels and short stories, he found poetry in the figures and tales of the past: both the historical and fabled, which were as vital to him as the present. Or rather, certain figures occupied an immanence in his mind, and they were haloed with an eternal presence, both secular and religious. Figures arise from Orkney's Norse tradition, and especially the early Christian martyr St Magnus, to whom Brown returns over and again throughout his life. (In 1961, the middle of a secularising century, Brown became a Roman Catholic.) He was adept at co-mingling past and present.

Freed from his 'surface complexities', Brown was able to develop his skills as a wonderful craftsman. Over the decades, he embraced and mastered new poetic forms, and his concerns deepened. But his intuitive grasp of image and symbol, and his ear for language which was apparent from the start remained unshakable. His writing voice is warm, rich and dramatic. He didn't employ a special 'poetry voice' – the same tapestry of sound is audible in everything he wrote: novels, letters and plays. Within his poetry, he could write ballads (and loved the Scottish ballads, with their fast, feudal, fate-driven compressed narratives). He could turn sonnets, such as 'The Old Women' and 'The Death of Peter Esson'. He had a pitch-perfect ear for free verse and yet could devise his own complex rhyme schemes. He wrote prose poems, such as those in *Fishermen with Ploughs* (1971), and his gift for image-making meant haiku moments came naturally. 'Sing' is a word he often uses, but 'dance' might better describe the way he conducts language. His rich lyric-world is a multi-handed dance, in which a whole sonic community is involved; his poems are like reels or strathspeys with no one excluded. To appreciate the luxury of his soundscapes, simply open this book at random, and read aloud. Or take the small poem 'Taxman', which is tucked within his major sequence *Fishermen with Ploughs*. The poem-cycle concerned the then deserted village of Rackwick on Hoy; Brown re-imagines its early settlement and abandonment.

TAXMAN

Seven scythes leaned at the wall.
Beard upon golden beard
The last barley load
Swayed through the yard.
The girls uncorked the ale.
Fiddle and feet moved together.
Then, between stubble and heather
A horseman rode.

Read closely, it becomes apparent that not one vowel sound, not one consonant lives alone. Each is announced then re-deployed throughout the poem. Take for example the poem's first vowel, the 'a' which occurs twice in 'Taxman', and which reappears in 'last' and 'barley' and 'yard'. Or the 'b' of 'beard' and 'barley' and 'stubble', or the 'o' in 'uncorked' and 'horseman', not to mention the alliteration, and the full and half rhymes. The sounds of the poem enact the cohesion and integrity of the community, and the harvest home dance they enjoy. Even the taxman is grudgingly accepted. We know that because he is brought into the weave of sound, the original 'a' of 'Taxman' recurring twice in the line 'A horseman rode.' And 'rode' completes the poem with a full rhyme on 'load', five lines before. No revolutionary moment here! It's a dance about a dance, every consonant or syllable, having been used, is let rest a moment before it is brought into play again. Like an Orcadian Strip the Willow. Or, if you prefer, tight-plaited as a corn dolly, made at harvest's end.

This rich aural quality can be traced from poets Brown admired, Keats and Hopkins, through to those who admired him: Heaney being the obvious one. This ear is evident throughout his prose too. Add to that a comfort with his native Orcadian speech rhythms, his Northern sensibility, and you have a unique poetic voice.

One of the pleasures of Brown's work is his 'accessibility'. If his work ever becomes 'inaccessible' it will not be because it is overly intellectual or theoretical – he abhorred that – but because his very objects, the homely wares of the poems, the poems' *nouns*, will become obsolete. Readers of the future may ask, 'What was a scythe? What was a tinker? A croft?' Being born in the 1920s meant that Brown witnessed the beginning of the end of an agricultural lifeway that had endured for centuries. Knowing that this lifeway was passing may possibly have given his work traction – as in his novel *Greenvoe* (1972). He wasn't ignoring change, as some claim, but agitated by it.

Or perhaps change was a mere 'drab surface complexity'. In an essay written for the St Magnus Festival in 1990, when he was in his sixty-ninth year and nearing the end of his life, Brown named four 'powers' which, he said, whether we like it nor not, condition our human lives. They are: Time, Fate, Chance and Mortality. He wrote, 'This is the use of poetry: to enable us to come to terms with those powers that cannot be denied, that surround us wherever we turn. We can actually hold a dialogue with them, through the medium of poetry ... it may be in the end we shall find the courage to turn and face them.'

And on his island gravestone, his own line is given as epitaph:

Carve the runes, then be content with silence.

Prologue

For the islands I sing
    and for a few friends;
not to foster means
    or be midwife to ends.

Not for old Marx
    and his moon-cold logic –
anthill dialectics,
    neither gay nor tragic.

Not that extravagance
    Lawrence understood –
golden phoenix
    flowering from blood.

For Scotland I sing,
    the Knox-ruined nation,
that poet and saint
    must rebuild with their passion.

For workers in field
    and mill and mine
who break earth's bread
    and crush her wine.

Go, good my songs,
    be as gay as you can.
Weep, if you have to,
    the old tears of man.

Praise tinker and saint,
    and the rose that takes
its fill of sunlight
    though a world breaks.

The Road Home

As I came home from Kirkwall
  The ships were on the tide:
I saw the kirk of Magnus
  Down by the water side:
The blessed brave Saint Magnus
  Who bowed his head and died.
His shining life was shorn away,
His kirk endureth to this day.
  As I came home from Kirkwall
  The ships were on the tide.

As I came home from Birsay
  A sower, all in tatters,
Strode, scattering the seed, immense
  Against the sunset bars,
And through his fingers, with the night,
  Streamed all the silver stars.
I watched him (leaning on a gate)
Scatter the glowing seeds of fate:
  As I came home from Birsay
  Against the sunset bars.

As I came home from Sandwick
  A star was in the sky.
The northern lights above the hill
  Were streaming broad and high.

The tinkers lit their glimmering fires,
    Their tents were pitched close by.
But the city of the vanished race
Lay dark and silent in that place.
    As I came home from Sandwick
    A star was in the sky.

The Storm

What blinding storm there was! How it
Flashed with a leap and lance of nails,
    Lurching, O suddenly
    Over the lambing hills,

Hounding me there! With sobbing lungs
I reeled past kirk and ale-house
    And the thousand candles
    Of gorse round my mother's yard,

And down the sand shot out my skiff
Into the long green jaws, while deep
    In summer's sultry throat
    Dry thunder stammered.

Swiftly the sail drew me over
The snarling Sound, scudding before
    The heraldic clouds now
    Rampant all around.

The sea – organ and harps – wailed miserere;
Swung me in fluent valleys, poised
    On icy yielding peaks
    Hissing spume, until

Rousay before me, the stout mast
Snapped, billowing down helpless sail.
        What evil joy the storm
        Seized us! plunged and spun!

And flung us, skiff and man (wave-crossed, God-lost)
On a rasp of rock! . . . The shore breakers,
        Stained chancel lights,
        Cluster of mellow bells,

Crossed hands, scent of holy water . . .
The storm danced over all that night,
        Loud with demons, but I
        Safe in Brother Colm's cell.

Next morning in tranced sunshine
The corn lay squashed on every hill;
        Tang and tern were strewn
        Among highest pastures.

I tell you this, my son: after
That Godsent storm, I find peace here
        These many years with
        The Gray Monks of Eynhallow.

The Exile

So, blinded with Love
He tried to blunder
Out of that field
Of floods and thunder.

The frontiers were closed.
At every gate
The sworded pitiless
Angels wait.

There's no retreat.
The path mounts higher
And every summit
Fringed with fire.

The night is blind,
Dark winds, dark rains:
But now his blood
Pours through his veins,

His hammer heart
Thuds in his breast
'What Love devises,
That is best,'

And he would not turn,
Though the further side
Dowered his days
With fame and pride.

What though his feet
Are hurt and bare?
Love walks with him
In the menacing air.

The frontiers sealed;
His foot on the stone;
And low in the East
The gash of dawn.

Rackwick
(for Ian MacInnes)

Let no tongue idly whisper here.
Between those strong red cliffs,
Under that great mild sky
Lies Orkney's last enchantment,
The hidden valley of light.
Sweetness from the clouds pouring,
Songs from the surging sea.
Fenceless fields, fishermen with ploughs
And old heroes, endlessly sleeping
In Rackwick's compassionate hills.

The Tramp

At the first shout of dawn he woke
And strung his boots, and scratched for fleas,
Dipped his face in the throbbing burn,
And wolfed his bits of bread and cheese.

There ran the road, his lord and master,
That he must follow to the end,
Whether it soared across a hillside
Or staggered past 'The Sailor's Friend.'

Sometimes through a summer cornfield
It made a rutty golden track,
Or broadened to a city street
Bearing a million on its back.

Nothing else mattered; he must follow
Although it brushed the lip of hell,
Or strode in stone across a torrent,
Or lingered round a village well.

And yet he is a king of space
Who measures space with his own feet,
And beast and sun and harvest field
Come dancing to his red heart beat.

from ORCADIANS, SEVEN IMPROMPTUS

Them at Isbister

Right on the very cliff verge
Is the croft of Isbister
And there old Janet lives
Who has borne four sons.

Two of them are under the hill.
One keeps a garage in Vancouver.
The youngest rarely comes home, being a sailor.

Old Janet has bright eyes
And thick brisk hands.
The parish dogs all know her.
She can tell the time by the sun
To within five minutes.

Now that Robbie is useless with rheumatics
Old Janet works Isbister.
Robbie sits by the fire smoking and spitting.
He welcomes any visitor,
Even the minister.

When Janet rails at Robbie
He rarely bothers to answer.
Sitting by the honeysuckle in July
Or under the tilley in December,

He is well contented.
He knows when it will rain
By the pains in his legs.

When a letter comes from the youngest boy
They peek at each other over their spectacles,
Spelling out the clumsy words far into the evening.

The dog barks in amazement.

When a butterfly knock comes at the door
Robbie says, 'Damn me, it's the minister.
But let him in.'

He gropes for his pipe.
Janet scurries to hang the kettle on the hook
And cries a welcome to the rattling sneck.

The Old Women

Go sad or sweet or riotous with beer
Past the old women gossiping by the hour,
They'll fix on you from every close and pier
An acid look to make your veins run sour.

'No help,' they say, 'his grandfather that's dead
Was troubled with the same dry-throated curse,
And many a night he made the ditch his bed.
This blood comes welling from the same cracked source.'

On every kind of merriment they frown.
But I have known a gray-eyed sober boy
Sail to the lobsters in a storm, and drown.
Over his body dripping on the stones
Those same old hags would weave into their moans
An undersong of terrible holy joy.

The Death of Peter Esson
Tailor, Town Librarian, Free Kirk Elder

Peter at some immortal cloth, it seemed,
Fashioned and stitched, for so long had he sat
Heraldic on his bench. We never dreamed
It was his shroud that he was busy at.

Well Peter knew, his thousand books would pass
Gray into dust, that still a tinker's tale
As hard as granite and as sweet as grass,
Told over reeking pipes, outlasts them all.

The Free Kirk cleaves gray houses – Peter's ark
Freighted for heaven, galeblown with psalm and prayer.
The predestined needle quivered on the mark.
The wheel spun true. The seventieth rock was near.

Peter, I mourned. Early on Monday last
There came a wave and stood above your mast.

Thorfinn

Sing Thorfinn's drowning.
                    Tired of his thieving guests,
The kestrel shape that wore his hand and eye,
The stealthy-by-moon deep-litter ghost,
And the seducer of vagrant Pertelotes,
Clad in his innocent hungers Thorfinn walked
Past farmyards havering with hens and greed.

Through streets of finger-pointing folk who'd set
Iron bars between him and the sun
(They shackled not the spectre but the boy)
Went Thorfinn to the clean curve of the oar.

Heart sick of the land
Where troubles grew with every grass blade
And every rose gushed from a septic root
And every casual car was the Black Maria,

He rowed his little boat behind the holm
To take the purple samurai of the flood.
Cornless they range, the lobsters.
By weeded rock and plangent pool
God puts in their beautiful claws
Sweet algae and tiny glimmering fish

The dropping surfeits of the rich Atlantic
Ravelling its rivers through the corn-patched Orkneys
And shrinking, twice a day.
(To their peril they eat man fodder:
Explore a casual fishgut hole, they're snared
In a tarry mesh, drawn up, and drowned with air.)
Whether it chanced, the Owner of these lobsters,
Grown sour at Thorfinn as any bristling poultry man
Turned a salt key in his last door of light;

Or whether Love, abroad in a seeking wave
Lifted him from the creaking rowlocks of time
And flung a glad ghost on a wingless shore:

No one can tell.
                            A crofter at early light
Found an empty boat stuttering on the rocks
And dawn-cold cocks cheering along the links.

Hamnavoe

My father passed with his penny letters
Through closes opening and shutting like legends
    When barbarous with gulls
    Hamnavoe's morning broke

On the salt and tar steps. Herring boats,
Puffing red sails, the tillers
    Of cold horizons, leaned
    Down the gull-gaunt tide

And threw dark nets on sudden silver harvests.
A stallion at the sweet fountain
    Dredged water, and touched
    Fire from steel-kissed cobbles.

Hard on noon four bearded merchants
Past the pipe-spitting pier-head strolled,
    Holy with greed, chanting
    Their slow grave jargon.

A tinker keened like a tartan gull
At cuithe-hung doors. A crofter lass
    Trudged through the lavish dung
    In a dream of cornstalks and milk.

Blessings and soup plates circled. Euclidian light
Ruled the town in segments blue and gray.
    The school bell yawned and lisped
    Down ignorant closes.

In 'The Arctic Whaler' three blue elbows fell,
Regular as waves, from beards spumy with porter,
    Till the amber day ebbed out
    To its black dregs.

The boats drove furrows homeward, like ploughmen
In blizzards of gulls. Gaelic fisher girls
    Flashed knife and dirge
    Over drifts of herring,

And boys with penny wands lured gleams
From the tangled veins of the flood. Houses went blind
    Up one steep close, for a
    Grief by the shrouded nets.

The kirk, in a gale of psalms, went heaving through
A tumult of roofs, freighted for heaven. And lovers
    Unblessed by steeples, lay under
    The buttered bannock of the moon.

He quenched his lantern, leaving the last door.
Because of his gay poverty that kept
    My seapink innocence
    From the worm and black wind;

And because, under equality's sun,
All things wear now to a common soiling,
    In the fire of images
    Gladly I put my hand
    To save that day for him.

Halcro

Don't go to that old man
With daffodil-shining dove-winged words
   To hang beside his clock.
His wall is wild with ships and birds.

Even the rum you bring
And the tobacco coiled and mellow
   He loves to chew, he'll stuff
In the oblivion of his pillow.

Give him the salty texts
Chanted in smithy, pub, and loan –
   How the corn's ripening; how
The pier was gray with Grimsbymen

Last stormy weekend; how
Sigurd got a pint of stout
   So riotously sour
They had to call the police out;

And how Grieg's spindly lass
With hollow neck and freckled brow
   Is suddenly grown a woman
And has two breasts like roses now. . . .

Then see his bone-bright hands
Frail on the chair, grow firm again
    In the stillness of old brawls,
Torn nets, sweet dust, and tangled grain.

Saint Magnus in Egilsay

Since Time folded his breath about the world,
Fixed in us wondering apes a praising tongue,
Strung his bright harps along the cold sea caves,
And broke our winter into grape and grain,
Plough, harrow, and scythe pressed on the virgin isles
Their circling kiss of peace. But one cold hill
      Locked thighs of stone against

The ardent ploughs, Penelope bound to a ghost.
They lured you there, a gentle enemy.
Bow your blank head. Offer your innocent vein.
A red wave broke. The bell sang in the tower.
Hands from the plough carried the broken saint
Under the arch. Below, the praying sea
      Knelt on the stones.

But O what love came then! Root, stalk, and flower
Twined in a riot through the acre of death
And larks cut lyrical nests deep in its turf.
Parched loin, and stringless tongue, and pearl-blind eye,
Sailed up that sound, fingered that dust, and saw
The red ploughs cleave their snow and curve for ever
      Across the April hill.

Elegy

The Magnustide long swords of rain
   Quicken the dust. The ploughman turns
     Furrow by holy furrow
      The liturgy of April.
    What rock of sorrow
  Checks the seed's throb and flow
Now the lark's skein is thrown
      About the burning sacrificial hill?

Cold exiles from that ravished tree
   (Fables and animals guard it now)
     Whose reconciling leaves
    Fold stone, cornstalk and lark,
     Our first blood grieves
  That never again her lips
Flowering with song we'll see,
      Who, winged and bright, speeds down into the dark.

Now let those risers from the dead,
   Cornstalks, golden conspirators,
     Cry on the careless wind
      Ripeness and resurrection;
    How the calm wound
  Of the girl entering earth's side
Gives back immortal bread
      For this year's dust and rain that shall be man.

Chapel between Cornfield and Shore

Above the ebb, that gray uprooted wall
Was arch and chancel, choir and sanctuary,
A solid round of stone and ritual.
Knox brought all down in his wild hogmanay.

The wave turns round. New ceremonies will thrust
From the thrawn acre where those good stones bleed
Like corn compelling sun and rain and dust
After the crucifixion of the seed.

Restore to that maimed rockpool, when the flood
Sounds all her lucent strings, its ocean dance;
And let the bronze bell nod and cry above
Ploughshare and creel; and sieged with hungry sins
A fisher priest offer our spindrift bread
For the hooked hands and harrowed heart of Love.

Daffodils

Heads skewered with grief
Three Marys at the cross
(Christ was wire and wax
festooned on a dead tree)

Guardians of the rock,
their emerald tapers touch
the pale wick of the sun
and perish before the rose
bleeds on the solstice stone
and the cornstalk unloads
peace from hills of thorn

Spindrifting blossoms
from the gray comber of March
thundering on the world,
splash our rooms coldly with
first grace of light, until
the corn-tides throb, and fields
drown in honey and fleeces

Shawled in radiance
tissue of sun and snow
three bowl-bound daffodils
in the euclidian season

when darkness equals light
and the world's circle shudders
down to one bleeding point
Mary Mary and Mary
triangle of grief.

The Funeral of Ally Flett

Because of his long pilgrimage
   From pub to alehouse
      And all the liquor laws he'd flout,
Being under age
      And wringing peatbog spirit from a clout
Into a secret kettle,
   And making every Sabbath a carouse,
Mansie brought a twelve-year bottle.

Because his shy foot turned aside
   From Merran's door,
      And Olga's coat with the red button
And Inga's side
      Naked as snow or swan or wild bog cotton
Made him laugh loud
   And after, spit with scunner on the floor,
Marget sewed a long chaste shroud.

Because the scythe was in the oats
   When he lay flat,
      And Jean Macdonald's best March ale
Cooled the long throats
      (At noon the reapers drank from the common pail)

And Sanders said
    'Corn enough here for every tramp and rat',
Sigrid baked her lightest bread.

Although the fleet from Hamnavoe
    Drew heavy nets
        Off Noup Head, in a squall of rain,
Turning in slow
        Gull-haunted circles near the three-mile line,
And mouthing cod
    Went iced and salted into slippery crates,
One skipper heard and bowed his head.

Because at Dounby and the fair
    Twelve tearaways
        Brought every copper in the islands
Round their uproar
        And this one made a sweet and sudden silence
Like that white bird
    That broke the tempest with a twig of praise,
The preacher spoke the holy word.

Because the hour of grass is brief
    And the red rose
        Is a bare thorn in the east wind
And a strong life
        Runs out and spends itself like barren sand
And the dove dies
    And every loveliest lilt must have a close,
Old Betsy came with bitter cries.

Because his dance was gathered now
   And parish feet
      Went blundering their separate roads
After the plough
      And after net and peat and harvest loads,
Yet from the cradle
   Their fated steps with a fixed passion beat,
Tammas brought his Swedish fiddle.

Shipwreck

Paul grounded at Braga, a gull on his shoulder.
The milkmaids wrung him dry.
He lay that night at the fire of Lifia
And then moved inland
And keeps pigs on a black hill.
    Jan put a cut of tobacco in his teeth
When the *Maggi* struck.
They found him at the end of the kirk
Near dawn, out of the gale,
Squirting poison among the tombstones.
    For Gregory was much grief in the crofts.
The sea did not offer him with green hands
To the seven dark shawls.
His bones fouled no net or slipway.
With small diagonals crabs covered him.
    Two storms and a dove later
A man with a limpet pail
Turned a gold swathe among seaweed.
That was the hair
Of Robin, weaver of nets, in a warp of ebb.
    Peero said when the first lump of salt
Fell through wrenched timbers,
'Now it seems I can never
Hang a brass chain at my belly
Or sit in the council

Or go among doors with the holy cards' . . .
The gray lumps fell and fell and stopped his mouth.
    Peter was three years getting home from the wreck.
He found his feet at Houton.
The ale-house there kept him a week.
He stayed at Gair for harvest,
Drowned and drunk again with broken corn,
Then shipped at Hamnavoe
For the blue fish, the whales, the Davis Straits
And casks of hellfire Arctic rum.
He stood dry in his door at last.
Merrag wore a black shawl.
He read his own tombstone that evening.
    For Donald the way was not long.
His father had a dozen horse at Skaill
But Donald loved the dark net.
Indeed for Donald the day and the way were not long.
Old men had said,
'Such skill at Greek and physics and poetry
Will bring this Donald fame at last.'
But for him the day was not long.
His day was this long –
Sixteen years, four months, and two days.

Horseman and Seals, Birsay

On the green holm they built their church.
There were three arches.
They walked to the village across the ebb.
From this house they got milk.
A farmer cut and carted their peats.
Against their rock
Fishermen left a basket of mouthing silver.
They brought the gifts of heaven
To the new children and the suffering shapes.
They returned to the island
And mixed their bell with the seven sounds of the sea.
Eight times a day
They murmured their psalms in that steep pasture.

A horseman stood at the shore, his feet in seaweed.
He could not cross over.
The sea lay round the isle, a bright girdle.
His voice scattered in the vastness
Though from shore to shore pierced cries of gull and petrel.
What did the horseman want?
Perhaps an old man in the parish was sick,
Or he wanted a blessing on his ship,
Or he wished to argue a point in theology.
From shore to shore they blessed him.
They trooped under the arch for nones.

After the psalms the horseman was still there,
Patient in the seaweed.
The sea shone higher round the skerry.
And the abbot said, 'Cormac, you are the carpenter
A blessed occupation.
And tomorrow you will beg some boards and nails
And you will build a little boat,
So that we do not need to keep horsemen waiting on the
    other shore
Who are in need of God' . . .

And while the boat was building under the crag
Paul gathered whelks.
From the cold triangular pools he gathered handfuls
And put them in his basket.
He sang *Dominus Pascit Me*, gathering whelks in the ebb.
Twenty seals lay on the skerry.
They turned their faces towards the psalm.
The brother sang for them also,
For the seals with their beautiful gentle old men's faces.
Then the ebb subtracted one sound
From the seven-fold harmony of ocean.
The tide lay slack, between ebb and flowing, a slipped girdle.
Paul gathered whelks and sang
Till the flood set in from the west, with a sound like harps,
And one by one the seals entered the new water.

The Poet

Therefore he no more troubled the pool of silence.
But put on mask and cloak,
Strung a guitar

And moved among the folk.
Dancing they cried,
'Ah, how our sober islands
Are gay again, since this blind lyrical tramp
Invaded the Fair!'

Under the last dead lamp
When all the dancers and masks had gone inside
His cold stare
Returned to its true task, interrogation of silence.

Farm Labourer

'God, am I not dead yet?' said Ward, his ear
   Meeting another dawn.
      A blackbird, lost in leaves, began to throb
And on the pier
         The gulls stretched barbarous throats
         Over the creels, the haddock lines, the boats.
      His mortal pain
         All day hung tangled in that lyrical web.

'Seventy years I've had of this', said Ward,
   'Going in winter dark
      To feed the horse, a lantern in my fist,
Snow in my beard,
         Then thresh in the long barn
         Bread and ale out of the skinflint corn,
      And such-like work!'
         And a lark flashed its needle down the west.

Old Fisherman with Guitar

A formal exercise for withered fingers.
   The head is bent,
     The eyes half closed, the tune
Lingers
     And beats, a gentle wing the west had thrown
     Against his breakwater wall with salt savage lament.

So fierce and sweet the song on the plucked string,
   Know now for truth
     Those hands have cut from the net
The strong
     Crab-eaten corpse of Jock washed from a boat
     One old winter, and gathered the mouth of Thora to his
       mouth.

The Year of the Whale

The old go, one by one, like guttered flames.
   This past winter
      Tammag the bee-man has taken his cold blank mask
        To the honeycomb under the hill,
         Corston who ploughed out the moor
      Unyoked and gone; and I ask,
    Is Heddle lame, that in youth could dance and saunter
        A way to the chastest bed?
The kirkyard is full of their names
        Chiselled in stone. Only myself and Yule
         In the ale-house now, speak of the great whale year.

This one and that provoked the taurine waves
   With an arrogant pass,
     Or probing deep through the snow-burdened hill
       Resurrected his flock,
        Or passed from fiddles to ditch
    By way of the quart and the gill,
  All night lay tranced with corn, but stirred to face
        The brutal stations of bread;
While those who tended their lives
        Like sacred lamps, chary of oil and wick,
         Died in the fury of one careless match.

Off Scabra Head the lookout sighted a school
  At the first light.
    A meagre year it was, limpets and crows
      And brief mottled grain.
        Everything that could float
    Circled the school. Ploughs
Wounded those wallowing lumps of thunder and night.
        The women crouched and prayed.
Then whale by whale by whale
      Blundering on the rock with its red stain
        Crammed our winter cupboards with oil and meat.

Hamnavoe Market

They drove to the Market with ringing pockets.

Folster found a girl
Who put wounds on his face and throat,
Small and diagonal, like red doves.

Johnston stood beside the barrel.
All day he stood there.
He woke in a ditch, his mouth full of ashes.

Grieve bought a balloon and a goldfish.
He swung through the air.
He fired shotguns, rolled pennies, ate sweet fog from a stick.

Heddle was at the Market also.
I know nothing of his activities.
He is and always was a quiet man.

Garson fought three rounds with a negro boxer,
And received thirty shillings,
Much applause, and an eye loaded with thunder.

Where did they find Flett?
They found him in a brazen circle,
All flame and blood, a new Salvationist.

A gypsy saw in the hand of Halcro
Great strolling herds, harvests, a proud woman.
He wintered in the poorhouse.

They drove home from the Market under the stars
Except for Johnston
Who lay in a ditch, his mouth full of dying fires.

The Hawk

On Sunday the hawk fell on Bigging
  And a chicken screamed
  Lost in its own little snowstorm.
And on Monday he fell on the moor
  And the Field Club
  Raised a hundred silent prisms.
And on Tuesday he fell on the hill
  And the happy lamb
  Never knew why the loud collie straddled him.
And on Wednesday he fell on a bush
  And the blackbird
  Laid by his little flute for the last time.
And on Thursday he fell on Cleat
  And peerie Tom's rabbit
  Swung in a single arc from shore to hill.
And on Friday he fell on a ditch
  But the rampant rat,
  That eye and that tooth, quenched his flame.
And on Saturday lie fell on Bigging
  And Jock lowered his gun
  And nailed a small wing over the corn.

The Sailor, the Old Woman, and the Girl

'Have you any help', cried the young sailor
Pulling against the tide,
'Have you any spell or herb to mend
This new pain in my side?'

The old woman gathering whelks
Raised her fierce gray head.
'The best cure in the world for that
Is, take her to your bed.

If watchdogs howl, there's two good places
To end a lover's moans –
The alehouse with its lamp and barrel,
The kirkyard with its stones.

Or use the black worm of the mind.
Think, when she leans up close
And all the lurings of Delilah
Break open like a rose

Against four eyes and throat and mouth,
That I am lying there,
Time's first lover stark as a thorn
In a white winter air'.

41

The girl sang from another shore
And the tranced oars beat on,
And the old woman's fingers went
Like roots through the gray stone.

Ikey on the People of Hellya

Rognvald who stalks round Corse with his stick
I do not love.
His dog has a loud sharp mouth.
The wood of his door is very hard.
Once, tangled in his barbed wire
(I was paying respects to his hens, stroking a wing)
He laid his stick on me.
That was out of a hard forest also.

Mansie at Quoy is a biddable man.
Ask for water, he gives you rum.
I strip his scarecrow April by April.
Ask for a scattering of straw in his byre
He lays you down
Under a quilt as long and light as heaven.
Then only his raging woman spoils our peace.

Gray the fisherman is no trouble now
Who quoted me the vagrancy laws
In a voice slippery as seaweed under the kirkyard.
I rigged his boat with the seven curses.
Occasionally still, for encouragement,
I put the knife in his net.

Though she has black peats and a yellow hill
And fifty silken cattle
I do not go near Merran and her cats.
Rather break a crust on a tombstone.
Her great-great-grandmother
Wore the red coat at Gallowsha.

The thousand rabbits of Hollandsay
Keep Simpson's corn short,
Whereby comes much cruelty, gas and gunshot.
Tonight I have lit a small fire.
I have stained my knife red.
I have peeled a round turnip.
And I pray the Lord
To preserve those nine hundred and ninety-nine innocents.

Finally in Folscroft lives Jeems,
Tailor and undertaker, a crosser of limbs,
One tape for the living and the dead.
He brings a needle to my rags in winter,
And he guards, against my stillness
The seven white boards
I got from the Danish wreck one winter.

from FISHERMAN AND BOY

Roads to the Kirkyard

Thorfinn, there are several roads to the kirkyard
Besides the way of the pillow.
There is the way of the west –
A few carry the salt key with them always.
There is the way of patriotism
But in the year of the foreign gun
Bilk and Drew and Howie
Ate limpets a whole winter in the cave.
There is the way of rum
That enchants the feet of twenty sailors
And bewitches one gravewards.
Before a girl kills you
Think of the rattling thorn on the brae –
Once it was crammed with roses.
Firth died among rafters – that noose
Had led his stallion through the nine parishes.
And Learmonth went over the crag for a ewe
And did not return.
The sheep afterwards had twelve winter lambs.

Each herring hangs at last by its own tail.

A House By The Sea

Thorfinn, build your house of quarried stone.

Josiah raised these holy walls, they say
For his lamp and bible
With red random rocks from the beach.
Then Kirsty came, who baked her sweet bread
For Breck and for birds in the snow.
Kolson the fisherman was here. The walls
Were white in the morning
And black when he sailed from the west.
Then a whole winter the walls were white.
Here Merran raised her seven bastards.
The close was never so gay.
She died young, of love and poverty.
Here Tom the tailor laid a long bench.
He stitched a coat for the laird
That later the scarecrow of Skarataing wore,
Dancing rags, half wind and half light.
Breck hung his fiddle on that wall.
After 'A Lamentation for Kirsty'
It died, sweet bird, among draughts and water.
Tinkers endured for one winter only
The spider's repairs
And the growing arrogance of rat and thistle.

Carve but one name over a lintel.

Good Ghosts

Thorfinn, I would not keep bread and ale
From any hunger at the door –
A patched coat may cover an angel.
When a ship breaks on the rock
Fold the drowned hands
Before the sand is strewn with rum and silk.
Do not neglect to wish him well
Who hoists a sail
Though formerly your words were crossed.
Lay an offering near the holy stones
Many men have straddled the boughs of Freya,
Keep yourself from those apples
Study the silence of the hawk.
You will find, seven good words
Over crossed hands
Will cancel much filth and evil from the ale house.

A fisherman has need of good ghosts.

The Drinkers

Thorfinn, to 'The White Horse' on Saturday mornings
The whalers come
Who end the day in a surge and fall of fists.
A few shepherds arrive at noon, peaceable men.
Fishermen come with scales in their beards
From the drifts of herring.
They generally sit in their own blue corner.
Then the ploughmen, after the lamp is lit,
With gaping bonnets and white collarless shirts.
Lords of the corn, they dominate the house
With fiddles and bawdry!
The whalers bear their resentment off, blue thunder,
To the rum barrels in *The Moby Dick*
(Rum is the drink for seamen).
Fishermen return to the piers of gull and herring.
The shepherds carry a gentleness back to the hills.
Only a tinker is left
Among the fiddles and the endless talk of horses.

Bread and ale, the sons of Barleycorn,
Study them well,
The dove's friend, the dancer with the knife.

A New Fishing Boat

Thorfinn, this new boat 'Whitemaa'
Can die as many deaths as a man.
Say two boards were badly fitted.
There are rocks like wolves all up the west,
Braga and Hellyan, Yesnaby, Marwick, The Brough.
A man and his boat like a sung word, a spell,
Compel the waters.
They dance well above the salt and the savagery,
The sudden swell that bursts from the sea's heart,
The wind that sweeps like an angel's wing.
These stresses break a bad song.
The 'Serpent' was cloven by a trawler.
The 'Swift' disappeared in shining seas, westward.
But that was a better doom than 'Thetis'
She lay in seapinks, turtled, a proud fisher
Decaying among hens.
Twelve years the nettles besieged her bursting sides.

Be the lonely cold questing eye of the gull.

The Fires of Love

Thorfinn, that the howdie* might cry
'A bairn clean and loud as a gull.'
That the old men and the young men might say
'This boy, I think,
Will throw a good net and hold his whisky.'
That girls might whisper
'Such a one could come to my bed and welcome'
That the merchants might say in their club
'This man owes nothing for twine
Or for hooks or meal or rum or a coat –
His name is a blank in our books.'
That an old woman might say
'He brought me to a house with fire and bed and cupboard,
A poor bright place.'
That the last road be grey with grief

Pray that your lust
Breaks to a red flame, then a white flame, before morning.

*Howdie – midwife

Places to Visit

Thorfinn, no man bides forever in one place
Like a cat or a pigeon.

In Birsay they move in their furrows, bread is broken
Half way to sacrament.
Here Magnus was born, here they laid his bones,
Here his first miracles came, seapinks
About a broken tombstone.
Hoy guards with its blue huddle of shoulders
An offering hand
That brims with corn and larks in June.
An Irish princess walked in the hall of Gairsay.
Egilsay keeps its broken kirk;
There one April were ploughs, nets, shawled women
And the rose of martyrdom.
Visit the circle of stones in Stenness;
Know then what a dark phallic sun
The martyrless Pict
Compelled upon his beasts and tillage.
A man talked with a mermaid in Deerness.
In Kirkwall a red pillar
Locks in the cloven skull of the saint;
Much curiosity, little sanctity;
A Godroot among dead stones.

Thorfinn, you will learn more in Orkney
Than Mansie did
Who made seven salt circles of the globe.

Whales

Whales blundered across us, threshing lumps,
Blue hills, cartloads of thunder.
They trekked between the ice and the hidden shoals.

In the west the gold whale sank in welters of blood.
We killed that ghost each sunset.
At dawn our hands were red and empty.
Now the *Dove* faltered out of the blind fist.

We notched barbs on various sticks and staves.
We spread the deck with lashings of salt,
Made harpoonman of herdboy.
'Heave her to,' sang the ribbed strenuous oarsmen.
The *Dove* dipped into the first whalequakes.

The women wondered at all these tons of love.
Gudrun crouched in the doveflank.
Every whale was a bolted slaughterhouse,
A winter of work for candle-makers.
The priest of Balder balanced a ritual point.
That sea was huge with sacrifice.
The *Dove* lappered in gules of sunset.

One thunderer rose athwart the spear rank.
The barbs broke on his bulk.

Sky jaw from sea jaw split, gigantic laughter!
His frolicking rudder deluged the *Dove*.
His mild lip sieved the waves.
He balanced a fountain southward on his skull.

Our fires slept in the golden jar.

Far back, those floating feast-halls belched.
Soon the stars flashed around like stalks of corn.

Witch

Three horsemen rode between the hills
And they dismounted at Greenhill.
Tall they stooped in at the door.
No long time then
Till Wilma came out among them, laughing.
The bible fishermen watched from the shore.
She sat behind the second dark rider.
They left the valley at noon.
And Wilma did not come back that day
Nor the next day
Nor any day at all that week.
And the dog barked lonely at Greenhill
And the girls took turns at milking her cow.
(One took the froth from her vat.)
The laird sent word
At the end of winter, to James of Reumin

That on Candlemas Friday
He should sail his dinghy to Kirkwall.
He sailed the *Lupin* to the red church.
And there at a steep place, Gallowsha,
Among tilted bottles, fists, faces
– A cold drunken wheel –
James saw the hangman put his red shirt on Wilma.

He sailed back smouldering
From the fire, the rum, the reproaches.
The dog of Greenhill
Barked in the throat of the valley.
And next morning
They launched their boat at the dawn with a wild shout,
The three unlucky fishermen.

Taxman

Seven scythes leaned at the wall.
Beard upon golden beard
The last barley load
Swayed through the yard.
The girls uncorked the ale.
Fiddle and feet moved together.
Then between stubble and heather
A horseman rode.

Shroud

Seven threads make the shroud,
The white thread,
A green corn thread,
A blue fish thread,
A red stitch, rut and rieving and wrath,
A gray thread
(All winter failing hand falleth on wheel)
The black thread,
And a thread too bright for the eye.

Ikey Crosses the Ward Hill to the Spanish Wreck

Because of the Spanish wreck I tackled the hill.
I heard of the apples,
Winekegs, mermaids, green silk bale upon bale.

My belly hollowed with hunger on the hill.
From Black Meg's patch
I plucked the loan of a curl of raw kail.

We both wore patches, me and that harvest hill.
Past kirk and croft,
Past school and smithy I went, past manse and mill.

On the black height of the hill
I lay like a god.
Far below the crofters came and went, and suffered, and did
    my will.

I wrung a rabbit and fire from the flank of the hill.
In slow dark circles
Another robber of barrows slouched, the kestrel.

Corn and nets on the downslope of the hill.
The girl at Reumin
Called off her dog, poured me a bowl of ale.

I found no silk or brandy. A bit of a sail
Covered a shape at the rock.
Round it the women set up their terrible wail.

A Jar of Honey

A woman came from every house that morning to the croft
of Scar. Slowly, like holy women, they moved through the
fields. Seven men stood at the end of the byre of Scar: five
young men, an old man, a boy. The oat fields were yellow,
gulls dipped and quarrelled over the mackerel in the bay. The
men stood outside the ceremony, unwanted and useless. One
of the young men shared the holy look of the women, but he
too was outside their ceremony. The other men did not have
a thing to say to him. They kept turning away from him. He
stood there in a double isolation. A woman with huge hands
and a face like stone crossed the fields, Bella of Windbreck.
She walked slowly, by herself. The door of Scar opened and
shut on this priestess. Now it was noon. The men at the end
of the byre smoked their pipes, all but the lonely one. Once
the boy chased a butterfly with a shout but the old man
checked him and the boy sat down at a fissure in the wall,
watching bees oozing out and in. A girl, an acolyte, crossed
over to the burn from Scar for water. With a pure white look
on her she passed the men and returned, silent and intent, a
heavy brimming pail at each side of her. Another woman
came out for peats, her arms red from the flame. The sun
dragged through the afternoon like an ox through furrows.
Suddenly the water girl stood in the open door of Scar, her
arms wild circles. 'Simon!' she cried. 'Come now.' The young
man turned his burnished face to the house. He wouldn't

move. He was afraid of the elemental women inside there, with their water and fire, the terrible priestess and her servers, swaddlers, shrouders, guardians of the gate of birth and the gate of death. He couldn't move. The other young men were laughing all round him now. They laid earth-coloured hands on him. They buffeted him gently. They turned his face towards the open door. Two of them walked with him, one at each side, to the threshold. He went inside alone. The boy sat at the end of the wall, gray wax at his mouth, his fingers threaded with honey. The old man knocked out his pipe, spat, lifted six creels from the wall, and slowly walked down to the boats.

A young man lifted a scythe from the end of the barn. He began to whet it on a red stone.

The gate of life had been opened.

Between that and the dark gate were the fish and the fleece and the loaf, the oil jars and the jars of salt and the jars of grain, and the one small jar of honey.

Ploughman and Whales

The ox went forward, a black block, eyes bulging,
The mouth a furnace.
Tammag went forward, cursing.
The plough wavered between them.
And gulls plagued Tammag, a whirl of savage snow
On the field of the sun.
Twice the plough struck stone,
A clang like a bell
Between the burning hills and the cold sea.
Tammag clawed his shoulder. He cursed.
And the ox belched lessening flame.
Six furrows now and a bit. . . .
Suddenly Tammag heard it, low thunder
Far in the firth,
And saw blue surging hills, the whales
On trek from ocean to ocean.
They plunged, they dipped, they wallowed,
They sieved a million small fish through their teeth.
The sun stood at the hill, a black circle.
The shore erupted with men and boats,
A skirl of women,
Loud dogs, seaward asylums of gulls.
The ox stood in the seventh furrow
In a dream of grass and water.
'Tammag!' the boatmen cried. 'Tammag!'

Tammag wiped his silver face on his sleeve.
He yelled at the ox. The plough wavered.
                                    They stumbled on.
They tore from the black sun
Loaf, honey-comb, fleece, ale-jar, fiddle.

Haddock Fishermen

Midnight. The wind yawing nor-east.
A low blunt moon.
Unquiet beside quiet wives we rest.

A spit of rain and a gull
In the open door.
The lit fire. A quick mouthful of ale.

We push the *Merle* at a sea of cold flame.
The oars drip honey.
Hook by hook uncoils under The Kame.

Our line breaks the trek of sudden thousands.
Twelve nobbled jaws,
Gray cowls, gape in our hands,

Twelve cold mouths scream without sound.
The sea is empty again.
Like tinkers the bright ones endlessly shift their ground.

We probe emptiness all the afternoon;
Unyoke; and taste
The true earth-food, beef and barley scone.

Sunset drives a butcher blade
In the day's throat.
We turn through an ebb salt and sticky as blood.

More stars than fish. Women, cats, a gull
Mewl at the rock.
The valley divides the meagre miracle.

Beachcomber

Monday I found a boot –
Rust and salt leather.
I gave it back to the sea, to dance in.

Tuesday a spar of timber worth thirty bob.
Next winter
It will be a chair, a coffin, a bed.

Wednesday a half can of Swedish spirits.
I tilted my head.
The shore was cold with mermaids and angels.

Thursday I got nothing, seaweed,
A whale bone,
Wet feet and a loud cough.

Friday I held a seaman's skull,
Sand spilling from it
The way time is told on kirkyard stones.

Saturday a barrel of sodden oranges.
A Spanish ship
Was wrecked last month at The Kame.

Sunday, for fear of the elders,
I sit on my bum.
What's heaven? A sea chest with a thousand gold coins.

Roads

The road to the burn
Is pails, gossip, gray linen.

The road to the shore
Is salt and tar.

We call the track to the peats
The kestrel road.

The road to the kirk
Is a road of silences.

Ploughmen's feet
Have beaten a road to the lamp and barrel.

And the road from the shop
Is loaves, sugar, paraffin, newspapers, gossip.

Tinkers and shepherds
Have the whole round hill for a road.

Butter

What's come of my churning? The van-man, he took seven pounds, and a basket of warm eggs, for jam, sugar, tea, paraffin. I gave the tinkers a lump, to keep the black word from our byre. I put some on the damp peats, to coax a flame. I swear the cat has a yellow tongue. There was only a scrape for the fisherman's bannock, like a bit of sun on a dull day. The old cow is giving me a mad look.

Natasha

The boat is wrapped round and about in swathes and cerements of fog. The people in the stern move like ghosts. But the petrel assures me that we aren't a cargo of dead people – it spurts out of the fog, it dips and hovers, it puts a sweet askance look over the *Truelove* and her voyagers. At least, though my violin is lost in The Black Flame – and all books and statues too, I think – we won't have to live in a birdless world. Yesterday I saw a seal or a porpoise, very indistinct, on the surface (or it could have been a bottle with the world's last message in it). The petrel again – it insists *This way! This way!* The men tug hard at the oars in rising sea, spindrift salts in, sifts in, Saul the Skipper throws an oilskin over the sack of seed corn. A chasm of purple sky – one cerement is lifted from our sea shroud, then dropped again, but a few stars pulsed like boys bathing (choristers in a rockpool). The petrel again – I love these birds, the lost cold drifting sea syllables.

The Five Voyages of Arnor

I, Arnor the red poet, made
Four voyages out of Orkney.

The first was to Ireland.
That was a Viking cruise.
Thorleif came home with one leg.
We left Guthorm in Ulster,
His blood growing cold by the saint's well.
Rounding Cape Wrath, I made my first poem.

Norway hung fogs about me.
I won the girl Ragnhild
From Paul her brother, after
I beat him at draughts, three games to two.
Out of Bergen, the waves made her sick.
She was uglier than I expected, still
I made five poems about her
That men sing round the benches at Yule.
She filled my quiet house with words.

A white wave threw me on Iceland.
Sweyn's skull is there (my brother) in a round howe.
Rolf rode him down
In Tingvoe, after the council, and rode on
Through villages, red-hooved, to the sea
Far from Inga his sister

And the lawless cry in the cradle, Inga's and Sweyn's,
And the farm at Rangower.
They put an axe in my hand, the edge turned north.
Women in black stood all about me.
There were lilies and snow on the hill above Broadfirth
And Rangower silent.
In Unst two nights, coming home,
We drank the ale and discussed new metres.
For the women, I reddened the axe at a dog's throat.

I went the blue road to Jerusalem
With fifteen ships in a brawling company
Of poets, warriors, and holy men.
A hundred swords were broken that voyage.
Prayer on a hundred white wings
Rose every morning. The Mediterranean
Was richer by a hundred love songs.
We saw the hills where God walked
And the last hill where his feet were broken.
At Rome, the earl left us. His hooves beat north.

Three Fridays sick of the black cough
Tomorrow I make my last voyage.
I should have endured this thing,
A bright sword in the storm of swords,
At Dublin, Micklegarth, Narbonne.
But here, at Hamnavoe, a pillow is under my head.
May all things be done in order.
The priest has given me oil and bread, a sweet cargo.
Ragnhild my daughter will cross my hands.
The boy Ljot must ring the bell.
I have said to Erling Saltfingers, *Drop my harp
Through a green wave, off Yesnaby,
Next time you row to the lobsters.*

The Coat

She bowed in her door, all ripeness.
The reaper went round and round.
Wave after wave of bread
Fell with a secret sound.
She sent the shuttle flying,
She laid the new cloth by,
And through that yellow spindrift
She sent a drowning cry.

With lie and crust and rag
Between two trees we move,
The drifting apple blossom
And the three nails of love.
Naked we come and we go.
Even the Incarnate One
Shed his seamless splendour
Under a sackcloth sun.

The old ploughman of Gyre
Laughed above his ale.
Lie after lie he stitched
Into a masterly tale.
He put down an empty mug.
The thread shore in *his* throat.
Between crib and coffin
You must dance in a beautiful coat.

Kirkyard

A silent conquering army,
The island dead,
Column on column, each with a stone banner
Raised over his head.

A green wave full of fish
Drifted far
In wavering westering ebb-drawn shoals beyond
Sinker or star.

A labyrinth of celled
And waxen pain.
Yet I come to the honeycomb often, to sip the finished
Fragrance of men.

Runes from a Holy Island

Press-Gang
    A man-of-war enchanted
    Three boys away.
    Pinleg, Windbag, Lord Rum returned.

Hierarchy
    A claret laird,
    Seven fishermen with ploughs,
    Women, beasts, corn, fish, stones.

Harpoonist
    He once riveted boat to whale.
    Frail-fingered now
    He weaves crab prisons.

Wreck
    The *Merle d'Or* struck at Scabra.
    One man flung shoreward,
    Cried strangely, fell.

Books
    No more ballads in Eynhallow.
    The schoolmaster
    Opens a box of grammars.

Skerries
> A fanged treeless island.
> On shipwrecked wood
> Men die, love, cry sunwards.

The Chapel of the Visitation
> Before the unuttered Christstone
> A new arch,
> Two bending women, a stone kiss.

Ruined Chapel
> Among scattered Christ stones
> Devoutly leave
> Torn nets, toothache, winter wombs.

Saint
> A starved island, Cormack
> With crossed hands,
> Stones become haddock and loaf.

Easter
> Friday, dayspring, a pealing cockerel.
> Haul west, fishermen,
> With flushed violent mouths.

Lost
> An island without roads.
> Ikey the tinker
> Stood throat-deep in the bog.

Dove and Crow
> A preacher broke our dove-stone.
> Sermons, crowflocks,
> Blackened furrow and shore.

Circle
    Cod, give needles and oil.
    Winter hands
    Must sew shrouds by lamplight.

Fish and Corn
    Our isle is oyster-gray,
    That patched coat
    Is the Island of Horses.

from THREE SONGS FROM A PLAY

The Ballad of John Barleycorn, the Ploughman, and the Furrow

As I was ploughing in my field
The hungriest furrow ever torn
Followed my plough and she did cry
'Have you seen my mate John Barleycorn?'

Says I, 'Has he got a yellow beard?
Is he always whispering night and morn?
Does he up and dance when the wind is high?'
Says she, *'That's my John Barleycorn.*

One day they took a cruel knife
(O, I am weary and forlorn!)
They struck him at his golden prayer.
They killed my priest, John Barleycorn.

They laid him on a wooden cart,
Of all his summer glory shorn,
And threshers broke with stick and stave
The shining bones of Barleycorn.

The miller's stone went round and round,
They rolled him underneath with scorn,
The miller filled a hundred sacks
With the crushed pride of Barleycorn.

A baker came by and bought his dust.
That was a madman, I'll be sworn.
He burned my hero in a rage
Of twisting flames, John Barleycorn.

A brewer came by and stole his heart.
Alas, that ever I was born!
He thrust it in a brimming vat
And drowned my dear John Barleycorn.

And now I travel narrow roads,
My hungry feet are dark and worn,
But no-one in this winter world
Has seen my dancer Barleycorn.'

I took a bannock from my bag.
Lord, how her empty mouth did yawn!
Says I, 'Your starving days are done,
For here's your lost John Barleycorn.'

I took a bottle from my pouch,
I poured out whisky in a horn.
Says I, 'Put by your grief, for here
Is the merry blood of Barleycorn.'

She ate, she drank, she laughed, she danced.
And home with me she did return.
By candle light in my old straw bed
She wept no more for Barleycorn.

Fiddler's Song

The storm is over, lady.
The sea makes no more sound.
What do you wait for, lady?
His yellow hair is drowned.

The waves go quiet, lady,
Like sheep into the fold.
What do you wait for, lady?
His kissing mouth is cold.

VIKINGS: THREE HARP-SONGS

Bjorn the Shetlander Sails to Largs 1263

I am a farmer from Yell in Shetland.
Bjorn my mother called me.
I grew among seals and clouds and birds and women.
The men came home in the ships for harvest
With wounds on them and bits of silver.
One year my father did not come home.
The sea has him, off Lindisfarne.
I learned drinking and love that winter.
I can handle horse or boat,
Useful crafts for a man to know,
And am thought to be a good chess-player
And passable on the harp.
Next year, if I live that long
My beard will have a fine golden curl to it.
Perhaps Thora will love me then.
I have never been further south than Whalsay.
Is it true, what the Vikings say –
Wine-skins, brothels, black faces south of Spain
And kirks colder than sea-caves?
This is good, to have seen fifteen summers.
Tomorrow with Paul and Sverr my brothers
I sail for Scotland.
A thousand sea-borne swords, a golden mask.

The New Skipper

Arn, Thorvald, Sven, Paul, Grettir, Harald
The *Sea Wolf* is out of the shed, new tar on her hull.
The rollers are under the keel.
The women have put ale, salt meat, and bread on board.
As soon as the wave runs clean from Birsay
We will leave the Orkneys behind us,
The scarred hills and the creeled sounds,
And tonight we will anchor at the mouth of a Scottish river.
Our voyage lies east this year.
We have heard of such towns – Aberdeen, Grimsby,
    London,
And the merchants who live in tall houses.
The churches have had enough of our swords
And the girls who weave their words into curse or spell.
Our voyage does not lie west this spring
Among holiness and drifts of rain.
There are few chalices left in those islands.
It is time the merchants knew about us.
We will be back in time for the corn harvest.
You women, see that the scythes are sharp and the barns
    swept,
And the ale thick with honey.
We are tired of broken coastlines.
This summer we deal in wool and useful currency.
They are not too beautiful, the girls in the east.

A Battle for Ulster

Remarking, 'It is not to my taste
To wheeze on a white pillow
Nor to toil graveyards on a stick, murdered slowly
By avarice, envy, lust,'
Einar ran where the swords fell thickest.

An Irish axe
Struck the right shoulder of Sweyn the skald.
'In future,' said Sweyn,
'I will write my poems with the left hand.
I will sup a sinister broth.'

Near the end of the battle
Rolf returned to the ship, downcast.
'Gudrun,' he said, 'is a proud woman.
She will not bed with boys.
Hard wounds I sought
For thigh and chest and forehead today.
All I have got
Is a broken tooth, an eye blue as an oyster,
And my pinkie scratched.
From now on, Gudrun,
I will court less particular girls.'

From Stone to Thorn

Condemnation
> The winter jar of honey and grain
> Is a Lenten urn.

Cross
> Lord, it is time. Take our yoke
> And sunwards turn.

First Fall
> To drudge in furrows till you drop
> Is to be born.

Mother of God
> Out of the mild mothering hill
> And the chaste burn.

Simon
> God-begun, the barley rack
> By man is borne.

Veronica
> Foldings of women. Your harrow sweat
> Darkens her yarn.

Second Fall
   Sower-and-Seed, one flesh, you fling
   From stone to thorn.

Women of Jerusalem
   You are bound for the Kingdom of Death. The enfolded
   Women mourn.

Third Fall
   Scythes are sharpened to bring you down,
   King Barleycorn.

The Stripping
   Flails creak. Golden coat
   From kernel is torn.

Crucifixion
   The fruitful stones thunder around,
   Quern on quern.

Death
   The last black hunger rages through you
   With hoof and horn.

Pietà
   Mother, fold him from those furrows,
   Your broken bairn.

Sepulchre
   Shepherd, angel, king are kneeling, look,
   In the door of the barn.

Bird in the Lighted Hall

The old poet to his lute:
'Bright door, black door,
Beak-and-wing hurtling through,
This is life.
(Childhood lucent as dew,
The opening rose of love,
Labour at plough and oar,
The yellow leaf,
The last blank of snow.)
Hail and farewell. Too soon
The song is mute,
The spirit free and flown
But you, ivory bird, cry on and on
To guest and ghost
From the fist stone
To the sag and fall of the roof.'

Sonnet: Hamnavoe Market

No school today! We drove in our gig to the town.
Grand-da bought us each a coloured balloon.
Mine was yellow, it hung high as the moon.
A cheapjack urged. Swingboats went up and down.

Coconuts, ice-cream, apples, ginger beer
Routed the five bright shillings in my pocket.
I won a bird-on-a-stick and a diamond locket.
The Blind Fiddler, the broken-nosed boxers were there.

The booths huddled like mushrooms along the pier.
I ogled a goldfish in its crystal cell.
Round every reeling corner came a drunk.

The sun whirled a golden hoof. It lingered. It fell
On a nest of flares. I yawned. Old Madge our mare
Homed through a night black as a bottle of ink.

Countryman

Come soon. Break from the pure ring of silence,
A swaddled wail

You venture
With jotter and book and pencil to school

An ox man, you turn
Black pages on the hill

Make your vow
To the long white sweetness under blessing and bell

A full harvest,
Utterings of gold at the mill

Old yarns, old malt, near the hearthstone,
A breaking of ice at the well

Be silent, story, soon.
You did not take long to tell

The Wreck of the Archangel

Who saw a rudderless hulk, broken loom of cordage
That nightfall? None. In the dregs of sun
    Westraymen had drawn high the yawls.
    They fed their byred lantern-lit cows.

Indoors, women tended the different flames
Of lamp and hearth. The old ones chanted again
    Mighty tempests of foretime.
    The children tumbled gently into sleep.

Then, under the lamentation of the great sea harp,
Frailty of splintering wood, scattered cries,
    The Atlantic, full-flooded, plucking
    And pealing on the vibrant crag.

Clifftop and shore thronged soon with lanterns,
The ebb strewn with spars and with drowned
    Foreign faces, but no breached cargo,
    Wine casks or baled Baltic furs.

And all lost, all drowned, a pitiful strewment,
Emigrants set forth to root poor lives
    On a free and fruitful shore,
    Skipper and crew with seaflock scattered.

(No, but spars and planks enough to keep
An island in roofbeams, tables, coffins, doors
   A century long – a quarry of wood.
   The jaw of sea at hull gnawing all night.)

A man listens. This can't be! – One thin cry
Between wavecrash and circling wolves of wind,
   And there, in the lantern pool
   A child's face, a dwindling, in seaweed tassels,

One only glimmer. The man turns from a sure quenching.
Probe and quest in the rich ebb. A girl
   Lifts the lost cry from the sea whelm.
   It breathes, cradled, at a kindled

Hearth, a thin cold flame. He endured there
The seventy ploughtimes, creeltimes,
   Harvests of fish and corn,
   His feet in thrall always
   To the bounteous terrible harp.

Fishermen in Winter

Such sudden storm and drifts
    We could see nothing, the boat
        Fluttering in a net
        Of reefs and crags.

The islands, blind whales
    Blundered about us. We heard
        The surge and plunge
        And the keening, all around.

Farm women had set stone lamps
    In the ledges that night.
        The village lamplighter,
        He had not thrown

Over the village his glimmering net.
    The skipper glimpsed one star
        – Soon quenched –
        But it beckoned to

A poor island with one croft.
    We moored *Fulmar.* We took
        Up to the croft door
        Two fish from the basket.

Island School

A boy leaves a small house
  Of sea light. He leaves
    The sea smells, creel
    And limpet and cod.

The boy walks between steep
  Stone houses, echoing
    Gull cries, the all-around
    Choirs of the sea,

Ship noises, shop noises, clamours
  Of bellman and milkcart.
    The boy comes at last
    To a tower with a tall desk

And a globe and a blackboard
  And a stern chalk-
    smelling lady. A bell
    Nods and summons.

A girl comes, cornlight
  In the eyes, smelling
    Of peat and cows
    And the rich midden.

Running she comes, late,
    Reeling in under the last
        Bronze brimmings. She sits
        Among twenty whispers.

Songs for St Magnus Day

1 The ship of Earl Magnus, going to Egilsay for a peace tryst, is struck by a great wave in a calm sea
'Steer the ship into this one steep wave.
But nothing matters more.
We have brought unwanted cargo, a jar of peace' . . .
Bailing pans flashed.
The comber struck the hull, and scattered the
    oarsmen, and flawed the jar.

2 Magnus foretells his death on Egilsay
Sailor, your heart is a stone bowl,
The wine gone sour.
A thistle will thrust daggers through that clay
On the trysted shore.

3 The sorrows of Magnus in the island of the church
If your good angel stands in a door
With a song of greeting, be sure
His dark brother is biding, silent, inside.
Today a long black coat stands at the pier.
The welcomer
Folds, with his cup of keeping, at a cold fire.

*4 Magnus passes a night in the church, and a Mass is said for
him in the morning*
So cold it is in the kirk
So dark this April night, in cell and choir
His hands dovetail
Like the one stone that locks an arch
To hold his shaken spirit still.
So cold it is, so dark.
Then, soon, the opening rose of dawn.
Calix sanguinis mei
One hand unfolds like a bird
And makes, at matin-time, a cross in the air.

5 Magnus comes out of the church and stands among his enemies
Ite: the voyage is over.
The skipper steps out of the stone ship
With a blank bill-of-lading.
A daffodil keeps a crumb of snow.
A lark
Soaks the 'isle-of-the-kirk' in a shower of lyrics.
He offers his clay to wheel and kiln once more.
Below, a ploughman
Follows, with a drift of gulls, his dithering share.

*6 The cook Lifolf is summoned by Earl Hakon to execute Earl
Magnus in a stony place*
Lifolf the cook had killed a lamb
And a brace of pigeons.
A shore-stone flowered with flames.
Lifolf gave the stewpot a stir.
Eight hawk-masks stood on the hill.
'Lifolf,' they sang, 'here's better butchering –
Come up, come up!' . . .

'The lords get hungry after a hunt,' said Lifolf.
He washed his hands in the burn.
He went in a slow dance
Up to the blank stone in the barren moor.

7 Invocation of the blind and the infirm at the tomb of Magnus
Saint Magnus, keep for us a jar of light
Beyond sun and star.

St Magnus Day in the Island

Now the door is opened. Now the bell
   peals thrice to summon the people.
They are there, outside, a disorder of voices,
     a babble.
'Enter silently and in order.'
Came first the brothers of Peter, seven fishermen,
   with a net, smelling of strong
   salt, the silver scales in their beards.
   Seven from *Fulmar* and *Otter*.
The bell rang.
Came the miller deaf from the thunder of great stones,
   and his dusty boy.
A peal, again. (I think the island trembled from
   end to end with the joy of that bell.)
They are not long down from the hill, the shepherds,
   from dragging ewes from the blizzard, folding
   new lambs from the east wind, breaking ice
   on the stiff burn. Summer will be a golden
   time for the shepherds. (No, daffodils
   wither also.) The old shepherd leaves his
   crook at the door.
Now the bell is a trembling silence. But the boys
   have begun their psalming.
I do not know how many poor people came into the
   church. There were many humble ones, they

kept well back, they wished to lose themselves
    in the shadows. The boy with the
    censer threw sweetness about them.
Open, everlasting gates, sang the choristers.
All outside make way for the laird, keeper of corn
    and peathill and jetsam, lord of the longship.
    The deacon sets him not far from the very poor.
    (All are grass and flowers of grass.)
A cloud covers the sun. The window darkens. The
    candles are suddenly bright. The young
    voices go on.
Welcome to the women in their gray shawls: who most
    endure, and have the silence of stones under
    sun and rain, but cry each upon other at a
    time of tempest and grief, stone upon stone
    shaken and huddled and harshly singing and
    each more precious than onyx or ruby. They
    are given honoured place. The lady Thora
    (the mother) is among them, neither the first
    nor the last. And one a daffodil breaking
    the bud, a child. And one with ashes about
    the mouth.
Is the bishop here? William, *senex*, will enter soon
    from the vestry.
The man of iron enters, dark from forge and anvil,
    smelling of soot and burnt water, strong
    from the tolling of his black bell, and his
    boy with him bearing horse-shoes.
The master of choristers turns a page, voices flutter
    like flames draught-flung. And resume,
    Who is the Lord of Hosts?
Now the boatbuilders, men of the adze and nails and
    the powerful keel, the caulkers, they that

98

curve the oars and make straight the mast,
they that send out seahorses to trample the
waves – the makers too of the little boats,
fish-seekers, that wither soon and break
upon rocks or are swallowed quick by the
Atlantic. They come, with cunning hands,
into the stone ship.
The doors must soon be closed. The doorkeeper holds
his place. Is there not room for sty-keeper
and beachcomber, the tinkers, and them that
rifle the rockpools for dulse and whelk?
There is room for all. They come in, one by one – a
knee seeks the floor, they rejoice with a
cross in the air like a shield going before
them.
Now a silence. Now there is silence, but for a jostle
and jargon outside – wherefore the doorkeeper
sets finger to mouth. The ploughmen. They
were late unyoking – the new field was stonier
than they had thought – late they were stowing
the ploughs in the lee of the barn. They come
in, one by one, the earth-workers, with the
sign of the earth: plough, and seed-sack, and
harrows, sickle and flail and winnowing fan.
The grieve from the Bu with a loaf and a
stone-jar, he is there.
Small cry of a bell at the altar.
The bishop comes in, with boys in white all about him.
The bread and the wine are set on the altar.
Dominus pascit me, sing the boys from the hill in the
choir.

The Jars

A house on the mist-shrouded moor! –
the ghost of a house

Over the lintel this carving
HOUSE OF WOMEN

Not a woman stirred, outside
or in

He knocked. No-one answered.
He pushed open the door

It was dark and cold inside
the house

He opened a cupboard. In the
cupboard was a small clay
jar with markings on it

He tasted the stuff in the jar:
finest of honey! His flesh
glowed with lost suns and
blossoms. He sipped again

Now the window was black
as tar

He stooped. He stroked with
blind hands the shape of a bed.
He covered himself with coarse
weave

He slept at once

The man woke. The window
was gray. He took down the jar
to taste more honey

The single jar stood on the shelf –
the shape of it had changed, and it
was of coarser clay

He opened it. It was crammed
with salt.

(The man heard, somewhere in
the house, a small cry)

He went through the rooms
of the house in search of a
child. The house was empty still

He returned to the room with
the cupboard and jar. He said,
*Young one, whoever you are, you
won't starve because of me –
There will be fish for the salting*

He came to a room where
the hearth was cold and the
lamp empty

On a stone of the wall was
carved the shape of a fish

He looked at the rune so long
that it seemed to pass into him
and become part of him

In another room, hidden, a
girl was singing

The man said, *Lost and
darkling creature, I will bring
you oil and driftwood
always*

The song guttered out. It
stopped. It faltered into
low cries of pain

The man wandered again
through the rooms of the house

He saw his reflection in a
pane. Furrows in the face,
a mesh of gray through his
black beard

A poor house, he said.
*There should be a bowl
on the sill, daffodils
or roses or heather, to say
what time of year it is – yes –
to spill some beauty into a*

bleak place. This jar is all,
it seems

He took the jar from the shelf.
An earth smell came out of it –
it was half full of flailed corn.
His hands that held the jar were
twisted with a summer of pain

Through the corridors of the
house a contented cry came. It
must (he thought) be a woman over
new loaves and ale, well pleased,
arms and face fire-flushed

Lost one in this house, he
said, *there will always be*
cornstalks – I will see to it

He scratched an ear-of-corn
on a stone beside the stone
with the carved fish

He lay down on the bed.
He was as weary as if he
had toiled, sunrise to
sunset, in a harvest field

He lay under a green and
a gold wave

His dream was about the
one jar that flowed always

from shape to shape, and
was ripeness, keeping, care,
sorrow, delight

    The man woke. He knew now
that he was old
    A thin-spun silver flowed over
the blanket. His hands were like
shreds of net, or winter roots

    Seven women of different
ages stood about his bed. They
all, from first to last, had the
same fleeting look: the lost
girl at the horse fair

    One by one, beginning with
the youngest, they bent over
and kissed him

    The mid-most woman smelt
of roses and sunlight. Her
mouth had the wild honey
taste

    The oldest one dropped
tears on his face

    Then the seven women
covered their faces and
went out of the room

He slept on into the starred
ebb of winter

He opened his eyes

A young man was
standing in the open door. He
carried a jar on his
shoulder

The young man greeted
him – then he turned
and went out into the
sun

The man said, *That is
my son. He is carrying
away the dust of my
death*

from POEMS FOR KENNA

A Writer's Day

GULLS
It was a long day in his field
Turning furrows like pages.
He strove towards a sign, the cornstalk.

THE INN
At noon he went to the inn.
Voices, smoke, shadows. He sifted
One heavy hard gleam from the gossip.

FISHERMAN
A fisherman came in, gale tangled,
With a basket of haddocks.
He struck a fish-shape in the stone of his mind.

CHILD
He met a child from the school, dawdling.
The wind
Strung gold across her quiet face.

GRAVEDIGGER
In the kirkyard, a spade
Knocked on the earth door.
In a croft, on the far side of the hill, a long silence waited.

SUNSET

His seaward window smouldered, black and red.
Would a poem come with the first star?
Lamplight fell on two white pages.

STRANGER

The latch lifted. A stranger came in
So beautiful
She seemed to be a woman from the sea.

Interrogation

How was the journey, man?
Darkness. A trudge in sun and wind and rain. Now, again,
   shadows.

What holds the line that curves upon itself, end to beginning?
   Can you tell?
A grave centre.

Lissomness stoops to dust. Plough and fiddle are
   dust. Children are tall distant dust. Love is
   dust of roses. Vanitas, grainings.
I honour the jar and the grains in the round jar.

Here's your door. Wait. Listen. Silence deeper than snow.
I accept the solstice.

What then, afterwards?
No more. The circle is closed.

The dance of clay goes on. You are not a memory any
   more among your waters and cornfields and skies.
   What then?
The millstone is quiet; then turns.

You are lost, man, among the atoms and planets.
I am content to be here beside a broken kirk
   where the poor have been fed.

from A SCOTTISH BESTIARY

Moth

The moth travels from pane to pane, in August
Wherever a lamp is set.

There's old Sammy playing his fiddle,
Such a rant
The sweet plea of the moth at the pane is lost.

In the next croft
Three children are reading their school books.
He thuds on the pane.
They are lost in labyrinths: seaports, poetry, algebra

Travel on, moth.
The wife is out in the byre, milking.
A fire-drowsed dog
Growls at the birring in the window.

Will nobody help a lost moth?
All he wants
Is a rag to chew, best of all
The golden rag in the lamp.

The moon is too far away.
In the next three crofts:

Ploughmen were drinking ale from a cog
And an old woman was knitting a sock
And a twisted couple
Were counting pieces of silver out of a sock
On to a scrubbed table.
They looked scared at the moth's delicate knock.
Ah, the fisherman is mending a creel in his shed
In a circle of light.
The moth enters on a sea-draught.
Ecstasy of flame
Hurls him to the floor, scorched.
And the fisherman says,
'Night-fly,
I wish the skate were as keen to come on my hook.'

The moth woke to ashes, dawn, a cold lamp.

Lobster

What are you doing here
Samurai
In the west, in the sunset streams of the west?

How you lord it over those peasants,
The whelks
The mussels and the shrimps and scallops.

There you clank, in dark blue armour
Along the ocean floor,
With the shadows flowing over you,
Haddock, mackerel,
And the sun the shadow of a big yellow whale.

Nothing stands in your way, swashbuckler.

The orchards where you wander
Drop sufficient plunder,
Mercenary in the dark blue coat of mail.

Be content, be content far out
With the tides' bounty,
Going from smithy to smithy, in your season
For an ampler riveting.

Fold your big thumbs,
Under the trembling silver-blue scales of the moon.

Raven

Nothing still: the west empty.
The sail useless in this north-westerly.
Sea too rough for the oars.
The raven in the wicker cage, he rages more than the
    seamen.
The seamen have their cheese and beer.
(For the raven, no food.
That raven hated us, through his bars).
Sun went down, russet.
'A good sign,' said the skipper,
But like all of us could hardly speak
For the shaking of his teeth.
We were cold men, from spindrift and hail showers.
A few stars came out
And they had the faces of children.
The young seamen slept.
I lay cold all night. The raven did not sleep.
The helmsman did not sleep.
Yet there is land in the west: Orcades, Alba, Ireland.
Raven screamed with hunger at dawn.
He screamed, seeing our oatcakes and beer.
Then sudden the wind swung nor-east,
The sail drank the nor-east
And *Seeker* went like a stallion over the gray field
    of the sea white-flowered.

He whose mouth was full of dooms
Pictured us galloping
Over the roaring edge of the world.
The young sailors, cheerful with the wind,
Laughed, and wind laughed,
And laughter of sea lay all about us.
(The starved raven, he laughed not.)
'Now let the raven go free.'
The boy unlatched the raven's cage
Cautiously, lest the raven have his eye.
But no, all thin as he was,
The raven leapt at the sun, and wheeled
High, and higher, and flung
His hollow eye round the horizon's ring,
And fluttered no bigger than a fly
Westward. Like a black arrow
The raven sped then into the empty west.
Then was our skipper glad.
Then he flung his arm about this shoulder and that.
'There is land there.
Our friend Raven has smelt worms and carrion.
Raven will be there first.
Seamen, keep your axes well honed.
There is land for us in the west,
Islands, fertile straths, mountains for goat pasture,
Fiords full of fish.
Boy, you shall have a sweetheart in Alba.'
One day still we followed the raven.
Then the helmsman pointed to a hill.

Whale

He has broken his boreal bounds, the whale.
Sea seethes about him
Like cauldron on cauldron of ale!

The rinsed eye of the whale
Sees, through spindrift and smother
A watchful wind-drinking sail.

A snow-cloud lours on the whale.
The armoured hide
Rebounds with volleys of sleet and ice and hail.

He pastures deep down, the whale.
The dreaming plankton,
Over his delicate lip they drift and spill.

He must breathe bright air, the whale.
He surges up,
A sudden fountain flowers from his skull.

What bothers him now, the whale?
A boatful of men.
He scatters them with a lazy sweep of the tail.

A harpoon has struck the whale.
And the barb quickens.
The iron enters him slowly, cell by cell.

Go to the lee of the berg, wounded whale!
He welters in blood.
The eye dims, and the foundry heart is still.

Eagle
The Child Stolen from the Harvest-field

An eagle, circling high.
The swaddled child
Lay in the bronze
Shadow of a barley stook.
The mother,
Bronze-throated, bent and gathered and bound.
The eagle
Hovered, stooped, threshed.
The child hung
Hooked in talons, dragged
Up blue steps of sky
To a burning nest
In a crag of Coolag hill.

The harvest mother
Followed. She changed
Burnish for blue wind,
Bleeding hands. She
Lifted the boy like an egg
From the broken
Circles of beak and claw and scream.
She brought him down
To her nest of crib and milk.
She kissed him.
She lit the lamp.
She rocked the cradle. She sang.

Old grand-da muttered
Through the gray
Spittle and smoke of his pipe,
'Better for the boy, maybe
That freedom of rock and cloud,
A guest
In the house of the king of birds –
Not what must come,
Ten thousand brutish days
Yoked with clay and sea-slime.'

John Barleycorn

I stirred in a cell deep underground
Blind, no taste or smell, no touch, no sound.

One day I slid the bar from the door.
I poked a pale nose into the air.

What was to be seen?
My hair and hands in the sun were green.

I saluted a canty old creature –
Mister Scarecrow, a stick and a tatter.

I was very poor, but then
I could dance to the pipe of the wind, the thrummings of
    rain.

The lark with its fluttering sky-weary breast
Was often my guest.

One morning I brightly awoke –
I was wearing a prince's yellow cloak!

I thought my dancing days would never be done
Under the sun.

A mud-coloured knave with a crooked knife
Stood before me, he threatened my life.

He severed me from my root.
He bound me hand and foot.

He beat the flesh from my bones.
In a double circle he trapped me, thundering stones.

O bitter hurt,
The graining and ooze of the heart!

'Can you sink, John, can you float?'
He scattered my dust in a seething vat.

The torturer
Finished his work with the red sign of fire.

In furrows born,
Forever I flush the winters of men with wassails of corn.

Rackwick: A Child's Scrapbook

The valley was a green jar,
   corn crammed

The green bowl
   brimmed with milk, honey, fish-oil

Once, the green jar
   tilted at sixteen hungry doors

Sealed in the jar now
   dust of old laughter and grief

They say, the jar flawed
   with heaviness of coins

Long fallen, the jar – shards
   half hidden in rushes

Hills tell old stories. Cliffs
   are poets with harps

Brightnesses broached –
   Shoal, peatbog, sheaves

Waver west, fish, with moon and stars.
   The sun's a cornstalk

   *

'Every day,' says the sea,
    'I count shell and wrack'

Stone in the burn
    counts millions of urgent waterdrops

The bum numbers
    roots, clouds, trout

'In my pocket,' says the cloud,
    'a thousand silver coins'

The rose
    spills incense and cold curls, a candle

Worm shares with lark
    charlock, broken gold
    *
'Soon now,' sang the peat,
    'I'll wear a red and yellow dress'

Welcome, eagle. That bird
    is home after a hundred years
    *
Buttercup, iris, clover
    idle in troops at the sun's door

Cornstalk cries, 'I'm the heir,
    first child of the sun-king!'

The shy worm, 'I toil
    in a cellar of the king's castle'
    *

Thugs are abroad with knives in July
   – clegs!

Yes, bandits too with rows of knives in their mouths
   – rats!

Midges in millions, at sundown, tapping
   cellars of blood

Mouse, clever thief
   unlocking stone to get to butter and candles

'No rose this,' sang
   the bee on the rusted barb

Has a lark
   slept in a bed of nettles, ever?

I wonder does the butterfly
   say *hullo* to the spider?

Listen – *plop*! – a trout
   has been gossiping with a cornstalk

Oh, bee
   to die in the heart of that rose . . .

The Horse Fair

Miss Instone said, 'Children, you were all at the Fair yesterday, I'm sure. Out slates! Out slate pencils! Write a composition on the following – My Day at the Fair . . .'

Twelve slate pencils squeaked and squealed on slate like mice in a barn.

Willie rubbed honey-of-sleep out of his eyes. He wrote.

I went to the Horse Fair.
I sat in the cart beside old Da.
In Dounby
We left Daffodil in the Smithfield yard.
A policeman was holding on to a man that could hardly stand.
Old Da gave me a penny and a farthing.
Old Da went into the inn.
I bought a bottle of stone ginger at an old wife's tent.
I saw hundreds and hundreds of people.
I saw Skatehorn the tramp.
Mr Sweyn went on with a long stick and a deer-stalker
And the women curtsied in his wake.
I saw Old Da in the crowd at last,
His face was like a barn lantern.
We stood and watched the tug-o'-war.

What red faces, bulging eyes, what staggerings!
It came on to wind and rain.
The whisky tent
Blew out like a ship in a gale.
Old Da had dealings with the blacksmith,
Nails and a new plough.
The blacksmith wrote numbers and words in a ledger after
    he had licked a small blunt pencil.
The blacksmith
Took a bottle and two glasses from a stone shelf.
He gave me sixpence!
We went home in the cart, Daffodil
Danced all the way.
She struck many stars from a stone.
The fiddler! – I nearly forgot the fiddler.
The whole Fair
Seemed to go round his fiddle. I saw a coal-black man
    stretched on a board of nails.
Three farmers,
Quoys and Graygarth and Longbreck,
Seemed like they had red patches sewn on their faces,
    coming out of the whisky tent.
Daffodil
Whinnied at the stars, 'What are you,
Nails or mayflowers?'
The moon was a skull.
Then the moon was bees and honey.
I woke up.
Old Da carried me out of the cart to our fire.

*'Spelling and punctuation need special attention,' said Miss
Instone. 'Few of you, it seems, had a really enjoyable day.'*

Sprinkling of water on eleven slates, rag rubbings, sighs,

Willie spat on his slate and wiped out that day with the sleeve of his gray jersey.

from STONE

Seascape: The Camera at the Shore

In the rockpool a child dips (shrilling)
Fingers, toes.

Below the widest ebb it opens,
The lost sea rose.

Then, drowning rose and reef and rockpool
The west inflows . . .

The Atlantic pulse beats twice a day
In cold gray throes.

Shy in a rock-caught crumb of earth
One seapink shows.

Scotland, scattered saw-teeth, melts like petals
In the thin haze.

Lucent as a prism for days, this shore, until
A westerly blows.

Then stones slither and shift, they rattle and cry,
They break and bruise.

Shells are scattered. Caves like organs peal
Threnody, praise.

Tangles lie heaped in thousands, thrust and thrown
From the thunder and blaze!

Silence again. Along the tidemark wavelets
Work thin white lace.

Among that hoard and squander, with her lens
Gunnie goes.

Stone and Star

The stone that sinks a creel
The stone that whets a scythe
The stone
That locks a bridge over the burn
The stone that keeps milk cold
The ordered stones that stand between hearth and a winter
    storm
The carved stone over the nest of skulls
The stone that children
Enchant to flower, ship, castle
The stone sea-vested twice a day
The stone the beachcomber
Strikes a match on to light his pipe
Between a crag and a stormfall,
A tall stone in a field
Strayed reveller from the circling Brodgar dance,
The seapink stone
The stone the ice Giant dragged out of Norway
The stone, Hesper,
That kisses a darkling ebbtide stone.

Shore Songs

The crab said, 'I'm locked in this pool
Until the Atlantic
Rolls back, and turns the blue key.'

The seapink said, 'I stand awhile
On a bare rock.
All summer I breathe salt and sun, then I die.'

The shell
To the child's shell-cold ear gives back
The innumerable choirs of the sea.

A driven ship in a gale,
A reef, a wreck.
'Here I lie, a piece of that kiss ever since,' the stone sang
    secretly.

Time a Stone

Storm and sea loss and sorrow is all
An old mouth at a rock

Tomorrow's wave will cover that boy and his yawl
An old mouth at a rock

Trust only the sweet clean water in the well
An old mouth at a rock

Let other girls wake to the black sea yell
An old mouth at a rock

Once I was lissom and sweet and tall
An old mouth at a rock

Fishermen hung sea silver at my wall
An old mouth at a rock

One lingered, fishless. My blood beat like a bell
An old mouth at a rock

I lit a lamp at a secret sill
An old mouth at a rock

A kiss is a cruel spell
An old mouth at a rock

A summer of kisses, then all goes ill
An old mouth at a rock

On the rosetree scents and petals sicken, they fall
An old mouth at a rock

Strength and goodness go under the hill
An old mouth at a rock

No songs but from the mouth of a child or a shell
An old mouth at a rock

And time a stone, and the feet of the dancers still
An old mouth at a rock

Song of the Stone

Said stone to buttercup,
'Dance till you're yellow rags, then die.'

Said stone to seagull,
'A broken egg, a chalky skull in a niche of a crag,
Not long, not long.'

The stone spoke to the man going with a plough.
'A mouthful of bread and ale,
Then the long sleep, under snow.'

Sang stone to star,
'Burn, cold candle. I wear after rain the swarming colours of
    day.'

Said stone to raindrop,
'Don't run.
We're for the mill, you and I, to grind bread.'

Stone in hourglass
Whirls, sighs, sinks upon silence.

The Lost Child
(for Edwin Muir)

They looked for him among the cornstalks.
He was not there.

In the field where the horses roamed
No sign of the child
Though one great plough-horse raised his head, listening.

Down at the shore
The limpet gatherers hadn't seen him.

'I think he'll be holding
An egg or a butterfly in his hand.'

He stoops to the bees and the clover.
A pure bead
Gathers, then falls forever through his thought.

I saw a boy chasing a small boy,
Their boots hidden
In little clouds of sun-dust.
The bronze of the school bell
Trembled around, like sword on shield.

That boy
Will trance a ship to the rim of the sea
Till his mother calls him.

Someone went in at the door of the green hill.
There the harp is,
Carved in stone among skulls and bronze helmets.
That rune will unlock
Time's labyrinth, door after door
To the tree and the apple.

The Coat
(for Edwin Muir)

In a croft door a boy puts on a coat
With a fish sewn on it
And a daffodil
And a great horse with a whirling hoof
And a quartered sun
And cornsheaves
And a high lonely hawk
And a seal on a rock –
The hem all stars and spindrift

The island women cover their heads on the shore

The boy in his coat of creatures, a Joseph
Journeys
Between the fifth and the sixth day
He lingers outside a tower

A gate opens. Seven iron masks
Consider the green coat.

Autumn Equinox

If you say, 'I am light'
I answer, 'Darkness'.
If you say, 'I tended the rose bush'
I reply, 'Frost flowers'.
If you say, 'A girl is reading a letter with parted lips',
I see a widow on the roads.
She knocks at a door. She has candles and needles to sell.

'A bird carries a burning seed
Into the blizzard.'

'The loom of time
Casts, this sunset, the year's third coat, harvest'.

We are sisters of a golden king.
We have travelled
One from the pole, one from the burning wheel
To a tryst on a doorstep.
I will light the lamp now in the west window.
You set the sun, as always, broken flames on the hearth.
We bide together one night, gladly, in the House of Man.
We go again, at sunrise.
One to the ice, one to the cage of fire.

The Twelve Days of Christmas: Tinker Talk

I saw the four shepherds, black
In the sun's ruin.
Four star-cut shadows, soon.

Folk going to Kirkwall to pay the tax,
Cart after cart.
We trailed behind, packs clanging.

I stood awhile at the shore.
Three ships
Quested by needle and hidden star.

Fire on the quarry-stone rooted,
A winter rose.
Butterflies of snow everywhere, a gray whirl.

Our donkey danders
Up small roads
To poor crofts. We offer cheap enchantments.

We chew limpets. Their peat smoke
Cures the sea silver.
A scatter, struck gold, over barn floors.

The islands white whales in the snow.
The rook on the branch
Had black thorns in his throat.

I thought I heard a night cry, a bairn
Poorer than me.
A white dream, surely.

In the street of Kirkwall
Talk of troubles.
Soldiers in the slush, kestrel-headed.

I saw the shepherds. One
Folded a shivering lamb.
They lingered at the door of the inn.

The sun was a shuttered hovel
Last time we passed.
Look now, new bright roofbeams!

We took pans and mirrors to Hamnavoe.
Three foreign skippers,
The pier heaped with bonded cargoes.

House of Winter

At last, the house of winter. Find
On the sill
Intricate ice jewellery, a snowflake.

Open one dark door. Wind-flung,
A golden moth! Soon
A candle flame, tranquil and tall.

It is a bitter house. On the step
Birds starve.
The sign over the door is warped and faded.

Inside one chamber, see
A bare thorn.
Wait. A bud breaks. It is a white rose.

We think, in the heart of the house
A table is set
With a wine jar and broken bread.

The Flute in the Garden
(to Judith)

January
    The flute sang
    Silently
    in the ear of a snowman

February
    A little white blossom
    unfurled
    through a stop in the flute

March
    The flute
    was washed in a wave of new green grass

April
    A daffodil danced in the wind, a splash of sun
    over
    the sleeping flute

May
    Small lyrics
    – daisy, buttercup, clover –
    covered the mouth of the flute

June
> Blackbird cocked a head at the flute, then
> trilled, questioned

July
> In the rosebush over
> the flute
> roses whirled, a white ballet

August
> A honeybee
> blundered across the silent flute
> – sweetness!

September
> Fall light, leaves,
> on
> Orpheus asleep in those chambers

October
> Waken the flute with a gift of apples,
> girl

November
> Can the flute
> follow her in to the fires and the lamp?

December
> Flute-song,
> star in the solstice tree

from *Brodgar Poems (1992)*

The poem sees the work on this Neolithic stone circle as lasting two or three generations at least. 'She who threw marigolds over you . . . is a crone now with cindery breath . . .'

It may have been a meeting-place, a temple, a hymn to the sun and the stars.

Even as a civilisation is being established, its history is beginning to crumble. Strange boats from time to time sailed along the horizon, going north and west, threatening the precarious settlements.

But a circle has no beginning or end. The symbol holds. People in AD 2000 are essentially the same as the stone-breakers and horizon-breakers of 3000 BC.

The Eleventh Stone
They say, never such loveliness between the lochs
As that girl.
In the pause between two stones
She became a swan.
She flew from us into sunset and stars.

The Thirteenth Stone
We have heard, men
Who have no knowledge of stones
Are in ships.
Save us, stone, from the harps in the west.

The Seventeenth Stone
They go, the old crones
Plucking heather
To thatch the huts before winter.
'Swan', they called one.
'Daffodil', one, once.
(The old men laugh)
'Dew of morning.'
'Butterfly.'
A new stone watches them.
They stoop, here and there, snatching.

The Twenty-fourth Stone: Thunder
Hammer on the hills,
Black stammer!
The cloud, a fistful of flashes,
Cut a stone forehead.
The stones, against the purple sky,
Danced.
After the thunder, sun.
One stone has a red wound.

The Twenty-eighth Stone
Curlew-cry
Across a clean stone face.
The old stones have lichen beards.

The Thirty-second Stone
She who threw marigolds over you, stone,
A child,
She is a crone now with cindery breath.
You, stone,
Two younger stones curve beyond you.

The Forty-fifth Stone
What broke from the cloud? Rain, sun, the hawk.
A stone walks under a cloud slowly.

The Fifty-second Stone
Look, a small boy with hook and limpet shell
Lying in the reeds.
The swan does not care.
The tall stone, if it cares, has care
Beyond the span of our caring.
Take seaweed from the boy's mouth.

Following a Lark

A Country Boy Goes to School

1

There he is, first lark this year
  Loud, between
That raincloud and the sun, lost
Up there, a long sky run, what peltings of song!
  (Six times 6, 36. Six times 7, 42
  Six times eight is . . .)
Oh, Mr Ferguson, have mercy at arithmetic time
  On peedie Tom o' the Glebe.

2

There's Gyre's ewe has 2 lambs.
  Snow on the ridge still.
How many more days do I have to take
This peat under my oxter
  For the school fire?
(James the Sixth, Charles the First . . . Who then?)
Oh, Mr Ferguson, I swear
  I knew all the Stewarts last night.

3

Yes, Mistress Wylie, we're all fine.
  A pandrop! Oh, thank you.
I must hurry, Mistress Wylie,
  Old Ferguson

Gets right mad if a boy's late.
I was late twice last week.
    Do you know this, Mistress Wylie,
The capital of Finland is Helsingfors . . .
        Yes, I'll tell Grannie
You have four fat geese this summer.

4
When I get to the top of the brae
I'll see the kirk, the school, the shop,
    Smithy and inn and boatyard.
I wish I was that tinker boy
Going on over the hill, the wind in his rags.

Look, the schoolyard's like a throng of bees.

5
I wish Willie Thomson
    Would take me on his creel-boat!
'Tom, there's been six generations of Corstons
    Working the Glebe,
And I doubt there'll never be fish-scales
On your hands, or salt in your boots . . .'

(Sixteen ounces, one pound. Fourteen pounds, one stone.)
A sack of corn's a hundredweight.
    I think a whale must be bigger than a ton.

6
Jimmo Spence, he told me
    Where the lark's nest is.
    Beside a stone in his father's oatfield,
    The high granite corner.

146

('I wandered lonely as a cloud . . .' Oh where? What then?)

I could go up by the sheep track
   Now the scholars are in their pen
And *Scallop* and *Mayflower* are taking the flood
   And the woman of Fea
Is pinning her washing to the wind.

I could wait for the flutter of the lark coming down.

7
The school bell! Oh, my heart's
Pounding louder than any bell.
   A quarter of a mile to run.
   My bare feet
   Have broken three daffodils in the field.

Heart thunderings, last tremor of the bell
   And the lark wing-folded.

'Late again, Master Thomas Corston of Glebe farm.
Enter, sir. With the greatest interest
   We all await your explanation
Of a third morning's dereliction.'

Maeshowe: Midwinter

Equinox to Hallowmas, darkness
    falls like the leaves. The
    tree of the sun is stark.

On the loom of winter, shadows
    gather in a web; then the
    shuttle of St Lucy makes a
    pause; a dark weave
    fills the loom.

The blackness is solid as a
    stone that locks a tomb.
    No star shines there.

Then begins the true ceremony of
    the sun, when the one
    last fleeting solstice flame
    is caught up by a
    midnight candle.

Children sing under a street
    lamp, their voices like
    leaves of light.

Crossing the Alps
Macbeth King of Scotland and
Thorfinn Sigurdsson Earl of Orkney

What should I say to Pope Clement?
  I do not know what I shall say
    Till the confession screen
Is there between us. Will it matter

If the Bishop of Rome doesn't understand
  My Gaelic, nor I his Latin?
    In truth, cousin, I hardly
Understand your Danish, but for

The courtesy and kindness that
  Flashes between us now and then
    Brighter than the high snows
We have ridden through since morning.

What should I say? I have killed a king.
  But in every court, from
    Scotland to India, powerful men
Stalk still like wolves in the forest

And Macbeth is marked in his turn
  For knife or poisoned cup.
    Besides, that king was weak
And the ordering of such beasts

Calls for puissance in sceptre and crown.
   The hands of the princes
      Frail as garden flowers.
Moreover, a nation needs a queen,

A strong mother to succour innocence.
   Sir, when I left Inverness, Gruath
      Walked many nights with a candle.
We will light heavenly candles for her

In the hundred churches of Rome.
   I have moreover this sack of pence
      To throw to the wayside poor.
Cousin, we have come to such friendship

On those perilous snow passes
   I know you will prevail on those
      Norwegian wolf-ships,
The men from the bays, Vikings, away

From our settled Scottish coasts, now
   I am threatened from south
      By the Saxons, from west
By the savages from Lewis and Argyll,

And your tables will never lack
   Salmon and Speyside usque
      Nor Ingibiorg your countess
Go without our cairngorms and silver.

Was there not Babel, the thousand
   Tongues? There's an angel
      Carries a heart's true sorrow
From penitent tongue to priestly ear

Urgent as the pleading of David's harp
   And the answer falls
     Purer than dew, silent
As manna in the desert. Look, cousin,

A gap of blue between the mountains.
   The groom goads the mule no more.
     Shall we halt beside this torrent?
The road winds down to orchards and vineyards.

To a Hamnavoe Poet of 2093

Language unstable as sand, but poets
    Strike on hard rock, carving
    Rune and hieroglyph, to celebrate
      Breath's sweet brevity.

Swan-path, whale-acre. Do you honour
    The sea with good images?
    We wear the sea like a coat,
      We have salt for marrow.

I hoard, before time's waste
    Old country images: plough-horse,
    Skylark, grass-growth,
      Corn-surge, dewfall, anvil;

Rain-trail from hill to hill, a hushing;
    Mayburn a penny whistle
    Lilting from Croval, lingering
      (Tinker-boy) under my window;

Creel-scattering gales; Thor's
    Hammer studdering,* on Hoy.
    Do your folk laugh and cry
      With the gentle ups-and-downs

* *studdering: reverberating*

Not so different, I think
  From talk in Skarabrae doors,
  Celtic shepherds at Gurness,
    Sweyn's boatmen off Gairsay?

The masque unchanging, the maskers
  Wear different motley.
  'Ox' is 'tractor' now
    On the green surge of Fea.

So, image maimed more and more
  On the grid of numbers
  Folk must not forget
    The marks on the rock.

Keep vigil. The tongues flow yet
  To rhythms of sea and hill.
  Deeper than stone, guard
    The pure source, silence.

from BLACK THORBJORN

'In Acre, sickness broke out in the ship's company, and many men of note died, including Thorbjorn the Black, Iceland poet'

Orkneyinga Saga

1

The best poets live in Iceland.
I have a farm there.
It is a long house – cows
Winter in one end.
   At the other end, barn and kiln.
I have been known to scythe hayfields.
   I've put a ring in a bull's nose.
   But men say, behind their hands
   'Thorbjorn with the black beard
Is the worst farmer in Broadfirth'.

5

I took two dowry mintings. I passed
   A week in a Reykjavik tavern
   Mostly drunk, with Ubi, Oddi, Arni,
   Poets from the fjords.

We sang, boasted, quarrelled.
   Ubi's harp a tangle of oak and wires at midnight.
'Good skalds are voyagers,
   Drinkers of gale and battle' . . .

'No, but the storm of images
Draws the mind beyond Rus or Markland
   Though the poet
Never leaves circle of lamplight' . . .

Then this sleaze of a taverner,
   'Thorbjorn, sir, the two silver pence
   Were exhausted
With the last clash of your ale-cups,

And Oddi, glacier poet
Has broken a valuable carved horn'.

St Peter and St Paul

1

Here where I write poems,
Three generations ago
A clerk
Wrote invoices in a ledger, concerning
    Consignments of 'Old Orkney' whisky.
He headed each letter
Stromness Distillery, June the 29th, 1900

2

The boats were in from the west.
    The seven fishermen
Had sold their haddocks along the street,
    Threepence a pound,
Weighing the fish on brass hand-scales.
The calendar
Behind Billy Clouston's bar counter
    Is ringed June 29.
Flett's ale is twopence the schooner
    To the scaled and salted fishermen.

3

An old blind man
Sits on a bench on a pier in the sun.
    He has thumbed his bible

Cover to cover, more than once
And he knows Peter
    Better than the famous whalers of his youth,
And Paul blinded with glory
On a road a bit like the road to Kirkwall
    (Not the drifting webs
    That dimmed his sea-wrinkled eyes)
But this summer day he doesn't see
    Today is the Feast of Peter and Paul.

4
Mrs Ross, postmistress
    Date-stamps her little flock of letters
'Stromness, 29 June 1900'.
    A postman – my father maybe –
Will take them in a sealed bag
    Down to the mail-boat *St Ola*.

And the birds will fly
    To Birsay, Edinburgh, St Johns, Sydney.

And Mrs Ross ponders letters with exotic stamps:
    'San Pedro', 'Sao Paulo'.

5
'This on the haddock's gills'
    Says Sinclair, fisherman, to a tourist
Sketching his boat and pier
'Is Peter's fingerprints'.

But Peter's fingerprint on the living silver
Is too small for the water-colour.

And Paul is a sea-echo only
To a far-travelled wealthy amateur artist.

6

Captain Halcro, skipper,
   Takes snuff, tells the minister
   Yes, indeed, he knows the waters
   St Paul sailed over, the rock
Paul shipwrecked on, in Malta.

Captain James Halcro
Has a very fine house behind the ramshackle town.
   He dines frequently
With Mr Rae at Clestrain and Mr Thom, Sheriff.

At each month's end
He visits Peter Halcro, fisherman,
   At the door they were born in, twins
Sixty-two years ago.

A pound. 'For twine, not rum, man . . .'

7

The kirk an old fisherman
   Will be buried from today
Is called St Peter's.

The globe-girdling ocean,
St Paul's waves peal forever
   On the beach below the kirkyard.

And tomorrow is the Feast of Peter and Paul.

Lux Perpetua

A star for a cradle

Sun for plough and net

A fire for old stories

A candle for the dead

*

Lux perpetua
By such glimmers we seek you.

Homage to Burns

1 Hebridean

'A book of poems is it?'
   Said the old man in Uist.
'When was it ever known
Songs between boards like caged birds?

Tell me more about this Burns –
   Has the wild rose
   Spilled over his hand ever, like heart's-blood?

The oppressor and the hypocrite,
Has he driven them, with bitter laughter, out of the glen?
Has he run his eye along ploughshare
   And broacher of blood, those edges?

But poetry should be given on the wind, like a lark or a
   falcon.'

2 Minister

Rev Wᵐ Clouston of Stromness:
One box books
From McCriven, booksellers, in the Canongate of
   Edinburgh.

The carter goes away with his fee.

Mr Clouston: 'Pope's *Iliad*,
Not a patch, I warrant, on the far-horizoned Greek,
But worthy the perusal.
Blair. Rousseau. Shenstone.
What, here? *Poems and Songs Mainly in the Scottish
     Dialect* . . .

Yes, Jane, the snuff-horn.
And light, if you please, that lamp on the table.'

3 *Skipper*
What, Simpson, what's that they're singing below?
What – repeat, please –
'A man's a man for a' that' . . .
There will be none of that Jacobinry on this ship.
Tell them, find better words.
A man
May be king or beggar, Simpson,
It's better so, every man
Locked in his place in the great music of society.
It was thus from the beginning of things.

A man's a man for a' that
On this ship a man is a sailor
And Simpson, I am the skipper.

4 *Bride's Father*
Lermontov. Byron. Burns.
The poets
Drop fruits from the great tree of poetry,
Lemon, pineapple, pear
And the roots locked in the hearts of men.
The Scotsmen,

161

Their poems are the wild sweet berries that purple the
    tongue.

Adieu for evermore, my dear . . .

Even here, in Petersburg
As the coach comes to take Nadia away.

5 *Sugar Planter*
'To Rob! Burns, Mauchline, Ayrshire, Scotland –'

There's no such place as Scotland more,
Write, 'North Britain'.

Has written poems, has he?

Rest assured, Mr Burns will write no poems in Jamaica,
Mr Robert Burns
Will be too taken up with account books, ledgers.
Here the black slaves do the singing.

Proceed 'Dear Sir,
We are in receipt of your letter of application of 16th ult' . . .

6 *Professor*
Was at the professor's last night, was he,
The rustic bard?
I thought Professor Blackie
Might open his door to worthier guests.

Here is one professor of law
Will not be entertaining
The wild warbler from the west.

Mr MacAndrew, listen.
The cloak of poetry is ancient and rich and jewel-encrusted.
It is not to be hung on a scarecrow between
The plough and the sickle.

7 *A Looker into the Seeds of Time*
In the starswarm is a world
In that world is a country
In that country is a mountain
In that mountain is a quarry
In that quarry is a stone
On that stone is a name

   The stone lacks chisel yet
   That quarry is unbroken yet
   The mountain has no root yet
   The country is the floor of a lake
   The world is a wheel of dust and fire,
   It turns
   Through chaos, blackness, silence.

   Now read the rune of the stone
   ROBERT BURNS POET

from *Daffodil Time*

1 DAFFODILS

Ho, Mistress Daffodil, said Ikey (tinker)
Where have you been all winter?
There was snow in the ditches last night
And here you are.
Did you light your lamp in that blizzard?

When Ikey came back
Next day, with his pack, from windy Njalsay
The yellow hosts
Were cheering and dancing all the way to the inn.

4 SCHOOL

In the island school
The children's heads
Are like green sheaths that will open soon.

And one of the seven shadows
Has left Mr McSween's face.

A lark glitters out song along the lift of the hill
And the bird
Is louder today than the chanted
Multiplication table.

And the globe of the world
In the dark corner, has a splash of light.

And Mr McSween says, like
A solemn son, 'This
Afternoon the Easter Holiday begins
But now, again – and better this tie – the three times
    table' . . .

And twenty-one faces
Open like daffodils.

Stations of the Cross: Veronica

Close your linen-shop, Veronica.
Who buys and sells
   The day a death-sentence is given?

This young man
I saw among the palms and shouting children!
   He must carry the dead tree.

He is not riding an ass today.
He is on his face, in swirls of hot dust.

A woman says his name
Like a mother that calls her child in from play.

He can't bear that baulk further.
A countryman slopes the burden across his shoulder.

I'm a quiet woman. But I took
A napkin I wove this morning
   To the blood, thorns, dust, sweat, on his face.

The centurion thrust me back. Six soldiers
Dragged him again to his feet.

There is weeping along the road.
The town women
Think of their sons, all the Sorrows of Man.

I would (but for the guardsmen)
Gather him up from the hot stones.

I would
Weave for such a one a coat of great beauty.

God created trees
For birdsong and fruit, not for this.

Tell me, sir – I can't read –
What is the writing on the tree?
  THE KING OF THE JEWS

Now the mother folds him home.
The child has never
Come back to such a sleep at evening, out of the country
    fields.

Go home now, Veronica, to your looms.
In a field outside the city
  See, a sower is burying seed in a furrow.

Stations of the Cross: The Good Thief

The cold Roman eye, hand on seal.
Vale. Take the thief away.

'You carry your own tree, Jimmy . . .'
Another gallowsbird behind.
One ahead, burdened, a bruised brightness.

I've carried millstones, wine-vats, a mast.
That one was a carpenter.
His knees buckle under the heavy baulk.

My mother, poor woman, is dead.
His mother is here. Poor woman. Poor woman.

Look, Simon's come into town
With an ox to sell.
They've laid another yoke on Simon.

Veronica, seamstress. No napkin ever
Soaked up such blood and sweat.

I stagger but I don't fall.
The sneak-thief plods like a mule.
The bright one, he's down again.

Those women! Miriam, Judith, Esther
Go home, sing over your cradles.
Sing among looms and pots.

Below, cornfields and vineyards.
A third time, fallen,
He tastes golden dust.

The soldiers won't bother, I think,
Haggling over my coat.
No scarecrow would wear a rag like that.

Silence – curses – from cross and cross.
From the mid-ark
A dove wings out into the blackest storm.
Thrust of lance into heart-root.
The soldiers are coming with mallets
To break the legs of the thieves.

The eyes of the mother
Drown all the world in pity and love.
The hammer beats on my knee.

That the hands of such a woman
Fold me gravewards,
Bear me and all men in her folds of light.

Robert Rendall
Orkney Poet

You have been here, before your latest birth,
   (Cheeks, at the pan-pipes, apple-red and round!)
Followed your wooden plough through Attic earth,
   And pulled your lobsters from a wine-dark sound.

Now for a flicker of time you walk once more
   In other islands, under geese-gray skies,
And note, on Birsay hill and Birsay shore,
   The year's glad cycle out of ancient eyes.

O happy grove of poetry! where the soul
   Is never sundered from the laughing blood,
But sweetly bound, harmonious and whole
   In covenant with animal and god.

But I came here unheralded, and meet
Masquers and shadows mingling in the street.

A Work for Poets

To have carved on the days of our vanity
A sun
A ship
A star
A cornstalk

Also a few marks
From an ancient forgotten time
A child may read

That not far from the stone
A well
Might open for wayfarers

Here is a work for poets –
Carve the runes
Then be content with silence

Lullaby for Lucy

Let all plants and creatures of the valley now
Unite,
Calling a new
Young one to join the celebration.

Rowan and lamb and waters salt and sweet
Entreat the
New child to the brimming
Dance of the valley,
A pledge and a promise.
Lonely they were long, the creatures of Rackwick, till
Lucy came among them, all brightness and light.

Stella Cartwright
(for her birthday – 15 May 1982)

So, once in the 50s
There was this crazy chap, high among clouds,
Edinburgh-bound.
Laurel-seeking he was, out of Orkney,
Long and salt his throat
Among the stanzas that starred the howffs of Rose Street.

Could he not bide forever in that beautiful city?
A sweet girl, one day,
Rose, a star, to greet him.
To him, she spoke sweeter than rain among roses in
    summer,

While poets like columns of salt stood
Round the oaken Abbotsford bar.
I, now
Going among the gray houses and piers of Stromness,
Hear that voice made of roses and rain still; and see
Through storm-clouds, the remembered star.

Saint Magnus

So, there was this knock at my door near the end of the night. I thought, 'Kurt the old man of Quoy is dying at last. Or, Brunna's child will be born at sunrise.'

I lit the candle. I took the bar from the door. A darkling stranger stood there.

He had the high-born chant. 'Mother, may I sit at your fire? Cold it was all night in the kirk. I want to sit at a croft fire for a while.'

The lord smelled of holy water, and sweat, and the salt of sorrow.

I pointed to the straw chair and the fire. I knelt. I blew the embers into a rage of flames.

I was shaken with rage against this lord. I whispered, 'Valt my son is dead. He went to your wars. He drowned in the sea at Sumburgh.'

The man said, 'The salt is over my mouth also.'

I said, 'Old Jon is dead because of you. Rents, taxes. He laboured harder than his ox. The last harvest broke him.'

He said, 'They have sharpened a scythe for me. I am near the mill and the millstones.'

I said, 'Here is not your place, sir. Go wherever you like. There are one or two stars still to light you through this island, to see what your wars have brought about.'

He said, 'You are an old woman. But you seem like a bride on the day before the wedding feast, flustered a bit with the ceremony to come . . . I will leave you now. Remember me in your morning prayer.'

I said, 'I get a smell of the ashes of death from you. I know that cinder. I have shrouded a hundred, men and women and bairns. I am happy to smell the ashes of the end on the breath of a war-bringer. Death was a friend to old Jon. I think Valt in your warship was not so pleased with his last mouthful of salt. Death is a thing of terror to the young and the rich and the great.'

He said, 'Remember me also when you light your candle to old Jon and young Valt.'

I said, 'Well, if death comes to you here in Egilsay, I will lay you out decently before the day is done, so your mother will sail here and look into the stillness of your face, and so come away again.'

He said, 'It will be for me a skull like a felled ox, a welter of blood and smashed bone. Even the rooks will stay far from it.'

The first light came in at the open door. The man's face was gray as a drained comb. I thought, 'This is a man that smelt of essence of roses yesterday and ate honey bread and had this and that spice in his French wine. He reeks like a shambles now. There is yet a kind of justice in heaven and on earth.'

I said, 'You will die today, I see that, like any hard-driven harvest ox or like a salt-throttled fisherman. I will put on a pot of ale for you to drink now. You must have a bannock with a bit of cheese and fish. A man shouldn't crawl to his end but stand up straight and look Death in the eye.'

We laughed together, like a harvester and a gleaner among the last sheaves.

His highness said, 'I thank you for your good cheer, mother.'
He made a cross with his hand upon the board.

We broke croft bread together.

It seemed that all the barley and meadowsweet and clover ever grown in Egilsay had come on the morning wind into my croft.

The lord of the Orkney glebes said, *Deo Gratias*.

He said, 'There is a square of brightness on your floor. It grows. The flagstone is warm. It is a sweet thing for the eye to behold the sun on a morning in April.'

Then on the doorstep Earl Magnus of Orkney kissed me on my withered apple of a cheek, a thing Valt never did for fear of fishermen's mockery, and old Jon did only when he was merry with ale at harvest home and Yule.

And here a fisherman passed on to the shore with his lines and there a ploughman was yoking his ox.

This death-farer fared on first to the kirk: to the Breaking of the Bread there, the first and the last Bread.

Soon there was a great stirring and shouting at the hidden end of Egilsay, and a smell of fires and stewing and grilling and a breached ale-barrel on the wind of morning.

'Magnus . . . Magnus . . . Magnus,' yelled the hidden hunters. 'Where are you hiding now, Magnus? Are you in a cave, Magnus? You can't bide forever in the kirk, Magnus. Come out soon, Magnus. Stand in the sun. Today, Magnus, we are all to sit down to a great feast.'

I threw the crusts that were left to my half-dozen hens.

The Harrowing of Hell

He went down the first step.
His lantern shone like the morning star.
Down and round he went
Clothed in his five wounds.

Solomon whose coat was like daffodils
Came out of the shadows.
He kissed Wisdom there, on the second step.

The boy whose mouth had been filled with harp-songs,
The shepherd king
Gave, on the third step, his purest cry.

   At the root of the Tree of Man, an urn
   With dust of apple-blossom.

Joseph, harvest-dreamer, counsellor of pharaohs
Stood on the fourth step.
He blessed the lingering Bread of Life.

He who had wrestled with an angel,
The third of the chosen,
Hailed the King of Angels on the fifth step.

Abel with his flute and fleeces
Who bore the first wound

Came to the sixth step with his pastorals.

On the seventh step down
The tall primal dust
Turned with a cry from digging and delving.

   Tomorrow the Son of Man will walk in a garden
   Through drifts of apple-blossom.

Song for St Magnus: 16 April

I

Keeper of the red stone, remember well
    Sufferers today, those
    Who are to cross the dark firth,
    People in hospitals,
    In hospices, eventide lingerers,
Children who look at daffodils
    (Both with the dew on) each
    To break today in spring tempest.

II

Consider, Magnus, the fishermen
    From Noup Head to Rora,
    Those with a hundred creels,
The old man with two creels behind the Holms,
    Consider a stranger at the shore
Who is in need of ferrying.

III

An Icelander wrote on his skin
   Death is darkness
   Death is the cold skull
   Death is the bitter journey all men take
   Into silence, nothingness . . .
The skald wrote. Music
   Moved across the parchment.

The dancer fared on to the stone.

IV

What you suffer at the stone, it has all
Been fore-suffered.
   We sit in an assize of shadows. Evil
Must be atoned for.
Whispers, beyond ear-reach
   Load us with shame and terror.

Heroic one, comfort us, you
Who have uncovered your head.

V

Magnus, friend, have a keeping
   Of the shepherd on the hill
   Whose ewes are having difficult birth
In the last snow.
Bestow peace to ploughmen in stony fields.

Be present at the fires
   Of women in Bosnia and Somalia
   Kneading dough smaller than fists.
Remember the Easter feast
   Your mother prepared in Holm
   You could not come to,
   Being finished with shadows.

The murderer came. He drank ale there, in Holm. He wept.

VI

Magnus, pray for priests
   In this time of hate
(Never such hate and anger over the earth).

May they light candles at their altars
This day and all days
   Till history is steeped in light.

It was a cold night, your vigil
   In the kirk in Egilsay.

At dawn an old priest lit the paschal candle:
   Introibo ad altare Dei

VII

Never so many strangers at Orkney's doors
   'We need peace' . . .
   'We are sent here about the business of government' . . .
   'Our quest: silence and healing' . . .

The old ways are worn out
We turn our hands to work on other looms.

Our ancestors
    Beat down the doors of Pict and Celt,
The people of Magnus
    Broke the first curraghs,
    Choked sacred wells,
    Filled barn and byre with flames.

Magnus, give welcome to strangers.
    Their children
    Will sing with new voices, in April,
    The words from the Iceland parchment.

An Old Man in July

I

Images grow slower on the worn loom.

    Lucent rain-bubbles
    Burst on the pools of his balcony
    And a sparrow
    Eyes from the rusted railing
    Bits of bread an old man scatters.

A blue sky patch – a scoured
    Silver coin eastward –
    A golden stone at noon.

No need for other pictures.

II

A burden: weaver, quarryman, poet.

    His house is crammed with books and manuscripts,
    Pictures, jars, music,
    One stone hollow heavy with coins.
    Better a bare cell in Eynhallow
    And a heart at peace.

III

Bairn-coat to shroud, the journey

    Near the end of the road
    The wind of before and after

Begins to shake the tatters of a man's life.

IV

'If only I was this sunset
Dear friend
Beside your fire, talking, proving
    The depth of your ale-mug . . .'

The quern of too many autumns
    Sifts dust of April into the urn.
All things indeed come from the hand of God
    But the random stone
    Is not thrid with our pain.

V

Think rather: the stone
    Ruins in sun and rain –
    Not ruins, it runs out
    Centuries long, fruitful or barren dust.

A wild stalk in a dry place
    Lifts into light.

A thousand winters on, somewhere
    A pilgrim mouth
    Will taste, thankfully or brutishly, the bread.

VI

This is true. Not wisdom or wealth can redeem
    The green coat, childhood.

Truth is, an old man comes
Led by a cold hand
To a hovel without a hearth-stone
    Empty cup, bare board.

On a wet morning, in an island
    An old man breaks a crust
    For a sparrow on a rusted railing.

VII

In the white theatre, autumn by autumn
A masquer takes needles to a torn coat

And the man must go out again
    Into deepening winter.

There is no skill or enchantment
    To make the old coat green.
    There can be at best, now
A flung or fated pattern of patches.
Stars pierce like nails, after harvest.

Near a hallowed stone
    The sparrow also builds her nest
    Introibo ad altare Dei

    Who giveth joy to my youth.

Norman MacCaig

Milne's Bar, Rose Street, Edinburgh –
A Saturday afternoon in 1956.

Sitting here and there about the unlovely tables,
Sydney Goodsir Smith, Tom Scott, Norman MacCaig,
    Robert Garioch, George Campbell Hay, Alexander Scott
And other bards
Whose lyrics, scratched on the backs of envelopes,
Would never fly into books.

A cry on the steps, 'Chris, he's here!'
And the bards rise to greet their king, Hugh MacDiarmid,
Just off the Biggar bus.

(This Orkney bard sits alone.
    He is too shy – as yet – to visit the bards' table.
Enough to look at them, with longing.
Their words have flown out of books
    To sit, singing, on the branches of his blood.)

And now, a few days since,
The last of those poets is dead,
MacCaig, he with the head of a Gaelic chieftain
And the courtesy,
His tongue an edged and glittering dirk

Against whatever is ill made, unworthy.
May the mountains
Gather about him now, in peace, always.

Haiku: For the Holy Places

Orc

    Orkney – 'orcs' – the school of sleeping whales,
    To those who glimpsed it first,
    Hills half-sunk in the sea.

Midsummer

    Midsummer, the hills wear fertile patches,
    Corn and pasture and meadow,
    Long green coats from the hills' throat to the shore.

The Northern Sky

    Orkney turns upon poles of light and darkness.
    A summer midnight, the north
    Is red with the two lamps of dawn and sunset.

Kirkyard

    Always, by the shore, kirk and kirkyard.
    The legends of the dead, their carved names
    Faced east, into first light, among sea sounds.

Wind

    Wind always, the unseen summer crystal
    Compelling boats, clouds, birds.
    The million whispers of fulfilment in the green ears.

Scapa Flow

Scapa Flow: great warships lie ramshackle
Under the gray floor.
And soon the veins of oil will throb and flow.

Sea and Cliffs

Sea, old sculptor, carves from the western ramparts
Stack and cave and skerry,
Sweep harpist, with sagas of salt and stone.

Fishing Bird

It waits, rock-fast, wind-flung
Wing – wind – enthirling
One flash from the sea's hoard.

Island Faces

Many masks merge here, in an island face –
Pict, Norseman, Scot
Face of a crofter, gnawed with loam
Face of fishermen, seamen –
Gray of the sea, eyes level as horizons.

Old Houses, New Houses

The old crofts ride the green hill surges,
Long arks; man and beast under one roof.
The new houses,
Will they be there at the dove's return?

Stromness

Stromness, Hamnavoe – 'haven inside the bay'
Twenty stone piers, with boats,
A street uncoiling like a sailor's rope.

Fishermen and Crofters

They hold the keys to earth and ocean,
Earth-key, the plough;
Sea-opener, the net and sinker;
Seventy years nourished with corn and fish,
They open the mysterious doors,
Go, most into earth,
A few through the door of the sea.
They gain the richness of man through the elements.

The Poet's Year

He can make his mouth chime –
Drops from a gray nail of ice

His silences
Are like the first cold root stirrings
His verse a trumpet in March
To widen the sun circles

Children come in a dance to his images:
Daffodil, lamb, lark

He wears the lyric coat
Cut from blue bales of sea and sky

He has knowledge of furrows
Beyond ploughmen

Can thrift sing, can herring?
He tongues their pink and silver silences

Sweeter than beeplunder, oozing,
The fairground fiddle

He knows the horncall, near sunset
For Hesper and Orion

He goes by stubble fields,
Tongue rich with shadows

He graves names of the dead
Deeper than kirkyard stones

What now, midwinter bellmouth?
Christus natus est.

Ikey: His Will in Winter Written

I, Ikey Faa, being of whole and sound mind, (nobody
    thinks it but me),
do hereby bequeath and leave my possessions
to the following persons, heartily praying that
those beneficiaries make full use
of the same, to their own hearty good and the
good of all the world beside.

Item: the birds of the isle, hawk and swan,
    eider and blackbird and dotterel, to the
    child JOHN SWEYNSON that gave me and the birds a
    bite to eat in last winter snow, and I in the
    high winds of March gave the said John a
    kite I had made out of sticks and paper for to fly among
      the
    said birds.

Item: the fish in the tides and rips and
    races about this isle, to JOCK SINCLAIR fisherman in
      the
    said isle: that he having to return the
    fattest fish to the laird's plate and kitchen, in
    exchange for a farthing or a halfpenny:
    since also the fingers of the laird have not baited hooks,
                       nor his lady's fingers

to my knowledge stunk with fish-guts,
and there is no true truce and tryst-time
as between hall and haul:
which season and compact are well
kent to the fishermen. I have had this and that cod-
     head
from John's goodwife.

Item: the flowers of the sun, from the first
       snowdrop to the last blown rose petal,
       to GERDA FLAWS, for I have not
       seen such delight in flowers in any
       house-bound creature, no, not in butterfly and
       bee; and I pray the said Gerda to
       ensure and guarantee all traffic as between
       bee and butterfly, sun and raindrop and
       the feast in the open bud. I wish for her
       a long happy butter-time and
       bannock-time and bairn-time, happy among flowers.

Item: I leave the land of this isle from the
       lowest rooted tangle in the ebb to the
       hawk over the hill to MANSIE GRAY and all others who
       changed it, in a thousand years and more,
       from a bog to a green-and-gold patchwork;
       and yet it wears Mansie Gray
       out, the land, it grinds him down and it
       grays him, bows and breaks him, to keep the big
       laird's house with nine empty echoing rooms and
       another in the city of Edinburgh; and forbye
       to stock the said dwellings
       with beef and bread and wine, silk and fiddles and
          etchings and harps.

I have eaten croft-crusts with thankfulness from Mansie
    Gray's table.

Item: The bums and the winds to millers.

Item: Rain and sun and corn to the makers of ale.

Item: to the factor a breath and a heartbeat and
    a breath, calculations, one at a time: as far as the last
        breath:
    such as are never noted among the ciphers and in the
        ledger in his office.

I, Ikey Faa, write this with a stick on snow and
mud in the quarry, three days before Yule,
having a hoast on me that does not
mend, and a fiercer burning in the
blood than I have known.

I have rejoiced greatly in the
elements that are soon to shake me out and away, all but
    earth – 'twixt
Yule and Hogmanay, as near as I can
guess – and I leave what is all mine and all men's and
    God's to them that
will enjoy and use it best.
As *Witness* – a sparrow (his splash in the ditch)
    a mouse (his scurry and snow mark)

(Will I manage to struggle to the ale-house
before closing time? If I do, will the thin-lipped
prevaricator that keeps the place give me the loan of a
last whisky?)

Index of Titles